Praise for 7 Magical Mushrooms

I implore you to approach this book and the alchemical world of mushrooms with an open heart and mind and prepare to experience The Best Day Ever!
   David 'Avocado' Wolfe - Author of 'Chaga: King of the Medicinal Mushrooms' & 'Superfoods: The Food & Medicine of the Future'

With the innate ability to connect to the plant and fungi kingdom, Juliette Bryant's immense knowledge shines through in her latest book on 7 magical mushrooms. She gives a deep insight into their medicinal and botanical properties alongside delicious recipes. This must have book is magical as Juliette delves into the folklore of mushrooms and her client's personal healing experiences show the life-changing and healing potential of mushrooms. Each page drew me ever closer to a holistic understanding of this wonderful species that grace our planet.
   Maria Wheatley – TV Presenter & Author of 'Divining Ancient Sites'

This refreshing book is comprehensive, informative and well-researched, unravelling both the mysteries and beneficial qualities of 7 specific mushrooms. It is a must-read for all those seeking to understand the folklore, mythology, healing properties and spiritual aspects of these 7 magical allies.
   Peter & Sue Knight – Authors of 'Albion Dreamtime'

Juliette's wisdom and passion of magical mushrooms oozes from the pores of this book. If you want to be transported into the mystical stories of the mushrooms, and get to know them as the guides they are; the blend of scientific, historical, anecdotal evidence and folklore will leave you feeling connected and confident in working with these mushrooms and their incredible powers. A must read for any health, spiritual or mushroom enthusiast.
   Melissa Amos - Author of 'Memoirs of a Mystic in Training'

Disclaimer

This book is for educational purposes only and is not designed or intended to be used to diagnose, treat or cure any disease.

Although mushrooms have been used as food and medicinally for thousands of years, consuming mushrooms has led to illness and even death. Always consult a health care practitioner before consuming mushrooms if you have any illness, are pregnant or breast feeding or on any medication.

If picking mushrooms out in nature, accurate identification is essential. Always cross-reference with an experienced mycologist and detailed field-guide. Some mushrooms are protected species and should not be picked in the wild. Some mushrooms are illegal to pick or prepare in certain countries.

This book is not designed as a detailed guide for identification. See the bibliography for suggested texts.

The author accepts no liability for any experimentation or harm caused by individuals actions based upon reading this book.

All of the client stories are real; however, names have been changed for confidentiality.

7 MAGICAL MUSHROOMS
JULIETTE BRYANT

TRANSFORMATIVE HEALTH PUBLICATIONS

Published - Winter Solstice 2024.

Transformative Health Publications.

Pear Tree Cottage, Stradishall, Suffolk, England, CB88YR.

www.juliettebryant.com

Text Copyright © 2024 by Juliette Bryant.
Images Copyright © respective owners.

All rights reserved.

ISBN: 978-0-9956041-5-5

Editing, text layout and book design by Giles Bryant.

Printed and bound in England by CPI Antony Rowe on FSC® paper.

This book is dedicated to my children
Samuel, Eliah & Zachary.
I love you all.

Contents

Acknowledgments / Photo Credits	8
Foreword by David 'Avocado' Wolfe	9
Introduction	13
The Magical Power of Mushrooms and the Mycelium Network	16
Why Do I Call Them "Magical "Mushrooms?	20
How Mushrooms Heal	23
7 Magical Mushrooms	
Chaga	34
Reishi	43
Lion's Mane	56
Turkey Tail	67
Cordyceps	81
Liberty Cap	91
Fly Agaric	107
Afterword – A Mycelium Meditation by Giles Bryant	127
Bibliography	130
About The Author	133

Acknowledgments

I would like to thank the wisdom keepers of the healing power of these magical mushrooms – both ancient and modern. I have learnt from many experts, both in person and through their writings, and I thank them all. The research and guidance of David 'Avocado' Wolfe has been particularly inspirational to me in writing this book, and I greatly appreciate him writing the foreword.

I would like to thank my husband Giles for working on this book with me in research, editing, design, layout, hunting for mushrooms and most of the photographs. Thanks to Ashley, Diana, Shannon and Leila for proof-reading. A big thank you to all of the wonderful photographers and artists who have kindly allowed me use their work in this book. I thank Roger Roberts for providing some useful technical advice.

Photo / Art Credits
Giles Bryant (All photography except by those listed below)
Amanda Sheldrake (www.amandasheldrakeart.wixsite.com 33)
Ashley Bryant (109)
Bethany Powell (119)
Ben Pearson (93, 105, 116)
Clive Hedger (www.clivehedger.com 28, 94, 126)
David Wolfe (11)
Emily Kirk (26, 59, 84, 86, 112)
Ethan Tizzard (32)
Faye Wingfield (106, 120)
Gina Metcalfe (front cover photo, 12, 19, 47, 55, 74, 75, 134)
Jenny Hill (91)
Jo McQueen (129)
Kaya Young (97, 125)
Marina Muttik (67)
Mark Phillips (back cover photo, 5, 107)
Peta Jade (70)
Robert Rogers (27)
Sam Walker (56)
Scott Courtney (78)
Zsuzsi Foroszan (www.tigerzsuarts.com 15)
Adobe Stock Images (34, 81)
Public Domain (30)

Foreword
By David 'Avocado' Wolfe

The journey into the mushroom kingdom often begins in the teenage search for nearby magical realms via magic mushrooms. That was likely how I became aware of the vast world of mushrooms in all their forms and types. Eventually, one's interest wanders deeper into the enchanted mushroom realms to discover a greater cornucopia of wonders than might be expected. The "magical" (psychoactive) mushroom exploration inevitably drifts toward the more subtle medicinal types of mushrooms. The breadth of this journey is covered in Juliette Bryant's unique book 7 Magical Mushrooms.

Today, various aspects of the mushroom world are at the leading edge of cooking, medicine, materials technology, computer learning, forest biology, human neurochemistry, biological communication, and so much more. Even as technological as all that sounds, just beholding the miracle of wild mushrooms growing out of your lawn, garden, orchard, local park, or the woods is truly - when looked at with a keen eye - inspirational. A book like this may be just the touchstone to pique your interest in what is quickly developing into a brilliant future where Nature's offerings of mushroom technology are more deeply integrated into human health and society.

As Juliette accurately points out, the great edible mushrooms of the world work primarily within several areas:
- Improving Immunity: Over time, the consistent consumption of medicinal mushrooms (teas, tinctures, mycelium, etc.) transforms human immunity.
- Nervous System Enhancement and Protection: One can improve the speed of wit and intelligence and nourish the brain and nervous system using both psychoactive mushrooms and medicinal mushrooms such as Lion's Mane.

- Adaptogenic: Living in the Canadian wilderness off and on for the last 20 years, I have discovered that wild medicinal mushroom teas contain some of the best adaptogenic qualities in all of herbology.
- Detoxification: Medicinal mushrooms have known capabilities to improve the function of white blood cells, which play a major role in detoxification.
- Nutrition: The mineral and nutrient content of wild mushrooms, such as chaga, is an important addition to a healthy and balanced diet.
- Spiritual & Emotional Healing: Psychoactive mushrooms may act as inner counsellors that show pathways to healing - of course, it is up to the individual to act on such advice.
- Synergising the Ancient Old with the Brand New: In some strange way, mushrooms of all types connect us to our ancestors, yet simultaneously show us numerous pathways for the future of civilisation.

Much may be studied, learned, and inculcated about the mushrooms of the world. Just start with the 7 in this book. From there, many tracks may open up for you with mushrooms, and remember this key one: observing them closely.

I have been in the health field for over 30 years. In all those years, nothing has come along that helps to heal one of humanity's deepest wounds - the separation from Nature and the natural world - better than mushrooms.

Mushrooms instigate. They activate us to move and get out and explore the Wild West of botany. Inspiration; illumination; information - no phone necessary. There is so much to discover. So much to find out. So much to investigate. And in the magical process of exploring the world of mushrooms, numerous pathways of healing are automatically invoked.

So, in summary, I implore you to approach this book and the alchemical world of mushrooms with an open heart and mind and prepare to experience The Best Day Ever!

David 'Avocado' Wolfe
Orator, Author, Organic & Biodynamic Farmer,
Adventurer, Meme Lord, Freedom Fighter
www.davidwolfe.com

Introduction

"The Earth is not a dead body, but is inhabited by a spirit that is its life and soul. All creatures, things, minerals included draw their strength from the Earth Spirit."
Basilius Valentinus

I am writing this book because these 7 magical mushrooms have helped me, my family and thousands of clients to achieve better health, mental clarity and personal transformation, sometimes in miraculous ways.

I have been called to share the wisdom and healing power of these amazing gifts of nature.

These 7 magical mushrooms have been used for thousands of years in cultures around the world. This wealth of anecdotal evidence about how they help to heal physical and mental illness, balance hormones, connect us to nature and find inner peace are now backed up by decades of scientific research and peer-reviewed studies.

In this book, I'll be sharing my personal journey with each of these magical mushrooms - their history, folklore, and traditional use including the latest scientific research showing their medicinal properties.

I have been making superfood products with medicinal mushrooms since 2008, and I'll be sharing some of my favourite stories from clients showing their healing power.

As a superfood chef and alchemist, I also share some of my favourite recipes and easy ways to use these mushrooms in teas, tonics, desserts and balms. Rest assured, you can do this safely and effectively – as people have done for thousands of years.

"Why only 7 mushrooms? Why these 7?" people have asked me. Well, these are some of my favourites, and represent a fantastic range of availability, healing power and pure magic!

This book is the culmination of a lifetime of wonder, research, experimentation and connection. It is my deepest wish that this inspires you to health and fulfilment.

Magical mushrooms have inspired humans for thousands of years

The Magical Power of Mushrooms and the Mycelium Network

"All things are connected like the blood that unites one family."
Chief Seattle

In the hidden depths of the earth, beneath our feet, lies one of nature's most extraordinary and interconnected systems - an intricate web that stretches across forests, fields, and even urban landscapes. This underground network, formed by the mycelium of fungi, acts as a vast communication system, connecting trees, plants, and other organisms in ways we are only beginning to understand. It is through this ancient and intelligent network that mushrooms not only thrive but also support and sustain life itself. The story of mushrooms and the mycelium network is a story of interdependence, co-operation, and the profound unity of all living things.

For millennia, mushrooms have held a sacred place in human cultures, revered as mystical tools with the power to heal, transform, and reveal deeper truths about the universe. From the medicinal properties of reishi, chaga, and lion's mane to the mind-expanding potential of psilocybin, mushrooms have long been associated with physical and spiritual healing. But beyond their individual abilities lies something even more profound: their connection to the vast, living matrix of mycelium, which sustains not only the fungi themselves but also entire ecosystems.

Mycelium is the vegetative part of fungi - a delicate, thread-like structure that forms networks under the soil, sometimes spanning entire forests. These networks are often referred to as 'nature's internet' because they allow trees and plants to communicate, share resources and support one another. Through the mycelium, older, stronger trees can nourish younger saplings and plants under stress can signal for help. In exchange for sugars from the plants, the mycelium provides essential nutrients and water thus creating a symbiotic relationship that benefits all life-forms within its reach. This is science, not science fiction!

This underground web is a vivid reminder of the interconnectedness of life. Just as the trees and plants rely on the mycelium to thrive, we too are part of an interconnected world, where every living organism plays a role in maintaining balance and harmony. The mycelium network teaches us that nothing exists in isolation - every action we take, every breath we breathe, ripples through the web of life, affecting the whole.

The idea of interconnectedness resonates not only in the natural world but also in the human experience. Like the trees that lean on the mycelium for support, we are also nourished by the relationships and communities we build. Our well-being is intricately tied to the health of the ecosystems around us. As we explore the magical power of mushrooms, we are reminded of our place within the web of life and our responsibility to protect and nurture it.

This book is a journey into the fascinating world of mushrooms and the mycelium network - a journey that reveals the magic of how life sustains itself through collaboration and connection. It is a celebration of the intelligence and resilience of fungi, whose invisible work beneath the surface enables forests to flourish, animals to thrive, and human beings to heal. By understanding the power of this hidden network, we can learn to live more harmoniously with nature, tapping into the wisdom of mushrooms to support our own health and the health of the planet.

In an age where disconnection from each other, from nature, and from our true selves seems to be at the root of so many of our challenges, the mycelium network offers a profound teaching. It reminds us that there is no separation between us and the natural world, that we are part of a vast, living organism that thrives on cooperation and mutual support. By looking to the mushrooms for guidance, we can begin to reweave the threads of connection, restoring balance and harmony both within ourselves and the world around us.

This is the magical power of mushrooms: not just their ability to heal our bodies, but their invitation to awaken to the deeper truth of our interconnected existence.

Just being with magical mushrooms is a powerful experience

I love collecting mushrooms in the wild

Why Do I Call Them "Magical" Mushrooms?

For me, and those who have worked closely with these mushrooms going back into pre-history, "magical" is a great description.

Looking at dictionary definitions, "magical" can mean:

"Beautiful or delightful in a way that seems removed from everyday life."

When walking in a forest and seeing a flying saucer shaped protrusion on an old tree, they are beautiful, delightful and seem far removed from everyday life. The experiences of those consuming psychoactive mushrooms, certainly can change people's perception of reality and lead to beautiful and delightful experiences.

"Having a special, exciting quality that makes something or someone different and better than others."

The mushrooms I explore in this book certainly have a special exciting quality that sets them apart from anything else on earth. Even the make-up of mushrooms is different than anything else: they are neither plant nor animal, but something mysterious in-between. And are they better than others? As we will see, in terms of their healing properties, some of these mushrooms are considered superior healing tools.

"Having special powers to make things happen that would usually be impossible."

Anecdotal evidence and modern scientific research from around the world show the incredible healing power of these mushrooms. They do indeed have special powers that can create changes in physical and mental health, the results of which, could be seen as impossible.

"Seems to work by way of some mysterious, unseen force."

Mushrooms do work in ways of a mysterious and unseen force, as the mushroom is the fruiting body of the great mycelium network that covers the planet – hidden below the surface but ready to appear (as if by magic) when conditions above ground are favourable.

It is believed that mushroom spores can survive in outer space. Some of the mushrooms on planet Earth, maybe some of the ones I'm looking at, may have arrived from another planet. Very mysterious indeed.

"Extremely or extraordinarily pleasant, enjoyable, or exciting."

And finally, I believe these mushrooms are indeed extremely and extraordinarily pleasant and enjoyable. Anyone who has had a superfood smoothie or super tonic tea with some of these mushrooms will know the feeling of wellbeing, calm and balance they bring. And are they exciting? Well dear reader, let's take a look and see……

Are some mushrooms from another world?

How Mushrooms Heal

"The sacred mushroom takes me by the hand and brings me to the world where everything is known."
Maria Sabina

Mushrooms have been revered for their healing properties for thousands of years, with their use spanning across various cultures and regions of the world. Some call them "medicinal" mushrooms, some "functional" mushrooms – but I like the term "magical."

From the ancient Daoist traditions of China to indigenous cultures in North and South America, mushrooms have played a vital role in traditional medicine and spiritual practices. In modern times, science has begun to catch up, with research revealing that many of the compounds found in mushrooms possess potent therapeutic benefits. In this book, we explore the healing power of mushrooms, focusing on their role in promoting physical, mental, and spiritual health.

1. Mushrooms as Immunomodulators

One of the most well-researched areas of mushroom-based healing is their impact on the immune system. Medicinal mushrooms like reishi, chaga and turkey tail are known for their immunomodulatory effects. These mushrooms contain compounds called beta-glucans, which help to modulate the immune system, either stimulating or suppressing it depending on the body's needs. This makes them useful in managing autoimmune conditions, infections, and even cancer.

For example, turkey tail has been studied for its ability to enhance the immune system's response to cancer treatments. In Japan and China, it is used as an adjunct therapy for cancer patients undergoing chemotherapy. The polysaccharide-K (PSK) found in turkey tail has been shown to inhibit cancer growth and improve survival rates in some studies.

Reishi, often referred to as the "Mushroom of Immortality" in Daoist texts, is celebrated for its ability to balance the immune system and reduce inflammation.

Sharing the wisdom of magical mushrooms is such a joy for me

2. Neuroprotective Properties and Cognitive Enhancement

Lion's Mane is a mushroom that has garnered significant attention for its potential to support brain health. In traditional Chinese medicine, it has long been used to nourish the mind and spirit. Recent scientific studies have revealed that lion's mane stimulates the production of nerve growth factor (NGF), a protein essential for the growth, maintenance, and survival of neurons. This makes Lion's Mane a promising natural treatment for neurodegenerative diseases such as Alzheimer's and Parkinson's.

In addition to its neuroprotective properties, lion's mane has been shown to enhance cognitive function, improve memory, and reduce symptoms of anxiety and depression. As modern society faces increasing rates of neurodegenerative disorders and mental health challenges, mushrooms like lion's mane offer a natural, holistic approach to mental well-being.

3. Adaptogenic and Stress-Reducing Qualities

Adaptogens are plants and/or mushrooms that help the body adapt to stress and restore balance. Several medicinal mushrooms, including reishi, cordyceps, and chaga, are considered adaptogens due to their ability to regulate the body's stress response. Chronic stress can lead to a host of health problems, including hormonal imbalances, weakened immune function, and digestive issues. Adaptogenic mushrooms support the adrenal glands and help mitigate the effects of long-term stress.

Reishi, in particular, is known for its calming and grounding effects. It is often used to promote restful sleep, reduce anxiety, and balance mood. Chaga, a mushroom native to the cold regions of Siberia and North America, has antioxidant properties that protect the body from oxidative stress, which is linked to aging and chronic diseases. Cordyceps, on the other hand, is an energising adaptogen that supports physical endurance and stamina, making it popular among athletes and those recovering from illness or exhaustion.

4. Detoxification and Liver Support

Mushrooms such as reishi and chaga are powerful detoxifiers, particularly for the liver. The liver plays a crucial role in filtering toxins from the body, and medicinal mushrooms help support this process. Reishi is known to protect the liver from damage caused by toxins, while chaga's high antioxidant content reduces oxidative stress in the liver.

These detoxifying properties make mushrooms important in cleansing protocols, particularly for individuals exposed to environmental toxins, heavy metals, or chronic stress. By supporting the liver's natural detoxification processes, mushrooms can help alleviate symptoms of fatigue, poor digestion, and skin conditions linked to toxicity.

5. Nutrient Profile

Mushrooms have a wide range of nutrients and can support our need for essential minerals, vitamins and antioxidant compounds. For example, chaga contains calcium, iron, zinc, B-complex vitamins, copper, manganese, potassium, magnesium and amino acids.
Many people still dry mushrooms in the sun and use them throughout the winter to help supply Vitamin D levels (although for me living in England, I wouldn't rely on this alone for my winter supply).

Did the consumption of magical mushrooms influence spiritual revelations?

6. Spiritual and Emotional Healing

In many indigenous and shamanic traditions, mushrooms are considered sacred medicines that promote spiritual healing. Psilocybin mushrooms, often referred to as "magic mushrooms," have been used in ceremonies for millennia. Psilocybin, the active compound in these mushrooms, is known for its profound effects on consciousness, offering deep psychological and emotional healing.

Recent clinical studies have shown that psilocybin has the potential to treat mental health conditions such as depression, anxiety, and PTSD.

By creating a heightened state of consciousness, psilocybin can help individuals confront deep-seated emotional trauma, process grief, and develop a greater sense of connection to themselves and the world around them.

Beyond its clinical applications, psilocybin has been used in spiritual traditions to facilitate experiences of oneness, transcendence, and communion with nature. These transformative experiences can lead to long-lasting changes in a person's sense of purpose, emotional well-being, and spiritual outlook on life.

In *Divine Mushroom of Immortality*, R. Gordon Wasson presents several arguments linking the Fly Agaric mushroom to the ancient ritual beverage, Soma. This drink was said to give people a special connection to the gods and the universe. Although we don't know exactly what Soma was made from, some researchers believe it could have included fly agaric.

The Rig Veda, an ancient Indian collection of Sanskrit hymns, frequently describes Soma using the term "hári," which translates to "flaming." Wasson interprets this as a reference to the mushroom's distinctive red cap with white spots, aligning with the vivid imagery associated with Soma.

Soma is described as originating from mountainous regions. Wasson suggests that this aligns with the natural habitat of fly agaric, which thrives in mountainous and forested areas, supporting the hypothesis of the mushroom being the source of Soma.

There are some other intriguing possibilities linking the fly agaric mushroom with certain symbolic or mystical elements in the Bible. These ideas, while speculative, explore how the mushroom's distinct appearance and psychoactive properties could have influenced ancient religious practices and texts.

Some theories suggest that the forbidden fruit in the Garden of Eden, often depicted as an apple, could instead represent fly agaric. The mushroom, with its striking red cap and white spots, has the appearance that could have given it a mystical or 'forbidden' allure. The experience of consuming fly agaric may also be seen as 'gaining knowledge,' which aligns symbolically with the tree that offered awareness of good and evil.

Stained glass from Canterbury Cathedral

In the Old Testament, "manna" is described as a mysterious food provided by God to the Israelites during their journey through the desert. The exact nature of "manna" is unknown, but its unique, almost magical appearance each morning has led some to draw a parallel to mushrooms, which often appear overnight. Fly agaric, or other psychoactive mushrooms, due to their ancient associations with shamanic rituals, are sometimes suggested as candidates for this "bread from heaven" that sustained people in times of need.

Another potential link is the story of the burning bush in the Book of Exodus, where Moses encounters a bush that burns with fire but is not consumed. Some interpret this as a metaphor for a transformative, spiritual vision. The vibrant red of fly agaric and its potential to induce powerful, visionary states may have been seen as "fiery" and was certainly transformative. This fits the description of an otherworldly phenomenon like the burning bush.

In certain medieval and early Christian art, some symbols, often linked to divine knowledge or enlightenment, resemble mushrooms, including depictions that look similar to fly agaric and also liberty caps. Some researchers argue that these representations suggest an esoteric knowledge of the mushroom's role in achieving altered states or spiritual communion, possibly hinting at early Christian communities who used it as a tool for mystical experiences.

These theories are hotly debated, but they invite us to consider how natural elements, like fly agaric and other mushrooms may have played a role in ancient religious traditions and texts. They offer a perspective that connects the human search for spiritual meaning with the natural world. When we examine most ancient cultures there are links to plants and mushrooms with psychoactive properties as gifts from the gods to allow deeper communion.

It can be argued that man's evolution has been influenced by the consumption of mushrooms, facilitating 'out of the box' thinking –

bringing about innovations throughout history. Some call this the 'Stoned Ape Theory'. Looking at more recent cultural influences, what would modern music be like without the psychedelic mushroom-influence of the music of Jimi Hendrix, The Beatles and Pink Floyd?

7. The Synergy of Ancient Wisdom and Modern Science

The resurgence of interest in mushrooms in modern society is a testament to their enduring power. While indigenous cultures have long known the healing properties of mushrooms, modern science is now providing the evidence that supports their traditional uses. This reinforces the convergence between the ancient wisdom preserved by shamans, yogis, sages and medicine people with modern science.

Although modern research on the medicinal aspects of mushrooms is only decades old, the results are very promising. They show that certain mushrooms, prepared correctly, can support radiant health and help heal disease. I present a selection of this research for each magical mushroom.

Conclusion

Mushrooms represent a bridge between ancient wisdom and modern science, offering profound healing potential for the mind, body, and spirit. From supporting the immune system to protecting the brain, detoxifying the liver, and facilitating emotional healing, mushrooms are a powerful tool in the pursuit of health. As research continues to uncover the vast array of benefits that mushrooms provide, their role in natural medicine will undoubtedly grow, offering hope for those seeking natural ways to heal and thrive in today's world.

Chaga
– The King of Mushrooms

Other names – *King of immortality, king of mushrooms, clinker polypore, diamond of the forest, black mass, Kabanoanatake (Japanese).*

Botanical – *Inonotus obliquus*

A hardened large black mass, chaga resembles burnt charcoal on the outside with a golden-brown colour on the inside. It can grow up to 50cm x 100cm in size like a massive eruption on the host tree. It favours cold climates and is mainly found in birch forests, growing all year round in northern climes such as Siberia, Scandinavia and Canada. It mostly grows on birch trees, with which it has a fascinating symbiotic relationship. What we see isn't the fruiting body, it is a highly condensed bundle of mycelium which has extracted the medicinal properties from the birch.

Historical Use

The name "chaga" comes from the word for "mushroom" in the Komi-Permyak, a language spoken by the indigenous people of the Ural Mountains in Russia. It is believed they were the first people to use these mushrooms medicinally.

Russian peasants would brew chaga into a tea called "Befungin", which was believed to strengthen the immune system, boost energy levels, and promote longevity. They also used it to relieve pain and inflammation and to treat digestive issues, seeing it as a universal remedy.

In North America, indigenous tribes such as the Inuit and Cree also used chaga as a natural remedy. They would harvest the fungus and brew it into teas or make poultices to treat various ailments, such as infections, respiratory issues, and skin wounds.

Indigenous peoples recognised the connection between chaga and the birch tree and believed that the fungus contained the healing essence of the tree. They used chaga in their healing rituals, believing it could restore balance and harmony within the body and connect individuals with the energy of nature.

In Traditional Chinese Medicine, chaga is known as "Bai Hua Rong" or "Hua Jie Kong Jun" and has been used for over two thousand years. TCM practitioners valued chaga as a superior herb for its ability to support overall health, balance the body's energy (Qi), and enhance vitality.

Folklore & Mythology

In Siberian shamanic traditions chaga is considered a sacred gift from the spirits of the forest. Shamans believed that chaga was given to humans by the forest spirits as a means to heal and protect. It was said that those who found chaga were chosen by the spirits, and if they used it with respect and gratitude, they would receive blessings of health and longevity.

It was believed that chaga grew only on ancient birch trees that carried powerful energies. These trees were seen as guardians of the forest, and the presence of chaga on them was considered a sign of the forest's protective and nurturing spirit. Finding chaga was viewed as a sacred encounter, an indication that the person was aligned with the natural world.

In Siberian and Russian folklore, chaga is sometimes called "The Black Heart of the Birch" because of its dark, charred appearance and its connection to the birch tree. The birch tree itself is a symbol of protection, renewal, and fertility in these cultures, and chaga was believed to be its spiritual heart - a concentration of the tree's protective and healing energy.

The story goes that when a birch tree reaches a certain age, the spirits bless it with chaga as a way of extending its life and sharing its healing power with humans. Consuming chaga was thought to allow a person to absorb the birch's strength and protective energy, thus ensuring vitality and resilience.

Chaga was used in rituals and ceremonies as an incense to purify and cleanse spaces, warding off negative energies and even evil spirits. Shamans believed that chaga had the power to connect them with the spiritual realm and enhance their abilities to communicate with ancestral and nature spirits.

In various myths, chaga is associated with the eternal spirit of the birch tree, a symbol of life, renewal, and fertility in Siberian and Russian cultures. It was believed that birch trees held the spirit of rebirth, and when these trees grew chaga, they shared their eternal energy with those who harvested and used it.

Some legends describe chaga as a portal to ancestral wisdom. In these stories, the spirits of the ancestors reside in the birch trees, and chaga serves as a conduit, allowing people to communicate with their forebears for guidance and protection. When used in ritual, chaga was thought to connect people to the wisdom of the ancestors, providing clarity and insight during important decisions.

Healing Properties

Antioxidant-rich, immune booster, anti-inflammatory, antiviral, supports digestion, reduces oxidative stress, skin health, liver protection, blood sugar regulation and enhances physical endurance.

My Story with Chaga

I first came across chaga mushrooms over 15 years ago, thanks to the writings of David 'Avocado' Wolfe. I was immediately captivated by its profound benefits. Alongside reishi, chaga was my entry point into medicinal mushrooms. Back then, I would enjoy simmering dried chaga chunks, reishi slices, astragalus root, and gynostemma into a nourishing tea that I would enjoy daily. I also used a chilled chaga tea as the base for my smoothies, which became a comforting ritual in my life. The feeling chaga gave me was one of uplifting clarity and a deep sense of being truly alive. Now I have made many of my own products with chaga as an ingredient, I use these instead.

Chaga came into my life around the same time I gave up caffeine, and it became a beautiful and sustaining replacement. At the time, I was a single mum of a little one and juggling four different jobs as I worked to establish my nutrition and wellbeing business. Chaga gave me a grounding I had never experienced before. In fact, this mushroom began to show me what it truly meant to feel rooted and present in the now on our beautiful planet.

I had always been someone who floated through life and struggled to stay grounded in the moment. However, when I started working with chaga, I began to learn the art of presence and being in the moment. These mushrooms awakened in me a deep remembrance of the sacredness of the earth and a profound reverence for the natural world. It was as though they helped me rediscover the beauty of being truly connected to this planet, and that connection has stayed with me ever since.

Anecdotal Evidence

Chaga features highly in traditional Siberian and Russian folk medicine, where it has been long revered as a healing tonic. Many people say that chaga tea or tinctures have significantly boosted their immune system, helping them fend off seasonal illnesses and even chronic conditions. It's often used by those with digestive issues, with individuals reporting improved digestion, reduced inflammation, and better overall gut health. There are also countless stories of chaga being used as a complementary remedy for cancer, particularly for its reported ability to reduce tumours and increase energy levels, and reduce sickness during chemotherapy.

In addition to its internal benefits, chaga has been noted for its skin-enhancing properties. Many anecdotal reports suggest that drinking chaga tea regularly or using it topically has improved conditions like eczema, psoriasis, and other skin irritations. People often describe feeling more balanced, energized, and grounded when consuming chaga, which they attribute to the mushroom's adaptogenic qualities that help the body cope with stress and environmental changes.

Scientific Research

Antioxidant and Anti-aging Effects

Chaga mushroom has one of the highest ORAC (Oxygen Radical Absorbance Capacity) scores among natural substances, indicating its powerful antioxidant properties. A study published in 2011 found that chaga extract significantly reduced oxidative stress in cells, which is a key factor in aging and disease.

[Study Reference: Mishra, S. K., Kang, S. C. Antioxidant activity of Inonotus obliquus. Mycobiology, 2011]

Cancer Prevention and Support

Research has shown that chaga contains compounds with anti-cancer properties. A 2016 study demonstrated that betulinic acid and other compounds found in chaga can inhibit the growth of certain cancer cells, including those associated with breast and colon cancer. The study suggests that chaga has the potential to be used alongside allopathic treatment.

[Study Reference: Park, Y. K., Lee, H. B., & Won, M. H. Anti-cancer potential of Inonotus obliquus. Journal of Ethnopharmacology, 2016]

Immune System Support

Chaga is well-known for its immune-modulating effects. A study published in 2018 revealed that chaga extract increased the production of cytokines, which are crucial for regulating the immune response. These findings suggest that chaga can help strengthen the immune system, making it beneficial for those with compromised immunity or chronic infections.

[Study Reference: Kim, Y. O., Han, S. B., Lee, H. W., Ahn, H. J., & Yoon, Y. D. Immunomodulatory activity of Inonotus obliquus. Mycobiology, 2018]

Anti-inflammatory Properties

Chaga has potent anti-inflammatory effects, as demonstrated in a 2014 study that examined its impact on inflammatory bowel disease. The results showed that chaga extracts reduced inflammation in the colon and improved symptoms in mice with colitis. These findings suggest potential applications for chaga in managing chronic inflammatory conditions.

[Study Reference: Lee, I. K., Yun, B. S. Anti-inflammatory effects of Inonotus obliquus extract. International Journal of Medicinal Mushrooms, 2014]

Antiviral Effects

A 2015 study found that chaga exhibits antiviral activity against several strains of viruses, including the hepatitis C virus. The study noted that chaga's antiviral properties are likely due to its high concentration of polysaccharides and betulinic acid, which help inhibit viral replication.

[Study Reference: Nakajima, Y., Sato, Y., & Konishi, T. Antiviral properties of chaga mushroom against hepatitis C. Phytotherapy Research, 2015]

A Client's Story

Daphne had been diagnosed with stage 3 breast cancer and had decided to treat her cancer naturally. She came to see me for a consultation. I advised her to make significant dietary and lifestyle changes, and to take a potent mushroom tincture alongside daily chaga tea. 6 months after following this protocol she was given the all clear from her cancer. 6 years later she is still cancer free.
Note: I am not claiming that mushrooms or the dietary and lifestyle changes 'cured' her cancer.

How To Use

Prepare as a tea by simmering chunks or powder in water from 45 minutes to 2 hours, depending on strength desired. You can re-use the chunks several times. Take an extract in the form of a powder or tincture. It has a mild, earthy flavour and can be consumed daily.

Featured Recipe - Chaga Tea

Ingredients:

- 1 small handful of dried chaga chunks (or 1tsp chaga powder)
- 4 cups of water
- ½ tsp gynostemma powder or leaf (optional)
- 1-2 tsp maple syrup, or coconut sugar (optional)

Instructions:

1. **Prepare the chaga:** If using chaga chunks, give them a quick rinse under cold water. If you're using chaga powder, no need to rinse.
2. **Simmer the chaga:** In a medium saucepan, add the 4 cups of water and bring it to a boil. Once boiling, reduce the heat to low and add the chaga chunks (or powder). Let it simmer for 45 minutes to 1 hour, or even longer if you prefer a more concentrated brew. The water will turn a deep, rich amber or dark brown colour.
3. **Add Cinnamon and Ginger (Optional):** If you're using gynostemma, cinnamon or ginger for extra flavour, add them during the last 10-15 minutes of simmering.

4. **Strain the Tea:** Once the chaga has simmered, strain the tea into a teapot or mug, removing the chaga chunks (or filtering out the powder and any spices).
5. **Sweeten (Optional):** Stir in maple syrup, or coconut sugar to taste. This is optional but helps balance the earthy flavour of chaga.
6. **Serve:** Pour the tea into your cup and enjoy! You can drink it warm or store it in the fridge for a refreshing cold tea.

<u>Contraindications for chaga</u>
There are reports of kidney stones and other medical conditions from constant consumption. Chaga may be contraindicated if on blood thinning medication.

Reishi
– The Queen of Immortality

Other names – *Soul mushroom, the Queen healer mushroom, Mannentake (10,000 year mushroom - Japanese), magic mushroom of the bedroom, Lingzhi (Chinese - spiritual potency).*

Botanical – *Ganoderma lucidum*

Comes in a variety of forms ranging from the classic flying saucer shape that clings to trees but some species look very different and can resemble the long fingers of a hand. Some species can grow up to 50cm across, though most are smaller. They like to grow on beech trees, but can be found growing elsewhere and they thrive in warm conditions. In the UK, there are 5 different types of Ganoderma that are referred to as reishi, all with similar botanical properties.

Reishi is a hard, inedible mushroom that requires preparation to extract its medicinal properties (see below).

Historical Use

In China, reishi has a history going back over 2,000 years. This mushroom has been cherished in Traditional Chinese Medicine for its purported ability to enhance longevity and improve overall health. In ancient China, reishi was highly valued by emperors, who considered it a symbol of divinity and longevity. This mushroom was believed to provide vital energy, restore balance in the body, and support the immune system. In Japanese and Korean cultures, reishi was similarly revered.

Throughout Chinese history, reishi was also viewed as a protective talisman. Some carried carved amulets resembling reishi mushrooms to ward off evil spirits and ensure good health. It was believed that the mushroom's power could not only protect the body but also shield the soul from negative influences.

Ancient Chinese texts, such as the *Shennong Bencao Jing* (Divine Farmer's Materia Medica), a classic of herbal medicine, mention reishi as a superior herb. It was noted for its ability to nourish the spirit (Shen), enhance life force (Qi), and rejuvenate essence (Jing).

Folklore & Mythology

In Chinese folklore, reishi is considered a divine mushroom, often associated with immortality and spiritual enlightenment. Ancient Chinese texts and art frequently depict reishi as a magical herb capable of bringing the dead back to life. It is said that reishi grows in remote, hard-to-reach areas, further emphasizing its mystical nature. Legends often tell of sages and hermits who ventured deep into the mountains in search of this rare and precious mushroom to achieve spiritual transcendence. It was said to grow in places where heaven and earth meet, making it a bridge between the earthly and celestial realms.

Reishi also holds a place in Daoist tradition, where it is believed to nourish the *shen*, or spirit. The mushroom is thought to harmonize the body, mind, and spirit, making it a staple in Daoist alchemy and practices aimed at achieving immortality.

In both Chinese and Japanese mythology, the deer is often associated with longevity, and it is believed that reishi mushrooms grow where the deer wander. This association led to the idea that consuming reishi not only extends life but also imbues one with spiritual insight and wisdom, akin to the mystical energy of these deer.

Healing Properties

Immune support, stress relief, anti-inflammatory, liver detoxification, antioxidant-rich, promotes sleep, cardiovascular health, anti-ageing, supports lung function and reduces fatigue.

My Story with Reishi

One of the most profound encounters in my journey with reishi occurred during a visit to a remarkable spice farm in South Goa called *Tanshikar*. This was many years ago, when I was still in the early stages of exploring these medicinal mushrooms. As we descended the steps into the heart of the farm, my breath was almost taken in wonder. In front of me, nestled in the natural landscape, stood a magnificent giant red reishi mushroom. It was the first time I had seen a reishi like this in its natural habitat, and my heart sang with pure joy.

This wasn't just a fleeting moment of excitement; it was something much deeper. The presence of the reishi had an immediate and profound effect on me. I felt an energetic shift, as if the mushroom itself was sharing its ancient wisdom with me simply through its being. The joy and awe I experienced weren't just intellectual - they were visceral, vibrating through my entire body.

This encounter taught me a lesson I would come to understand more fully over time: we do not always need to consume a plant or mushroom to experience its healing properties. Everything is vibration. Just as we can feel the warmth of the sun without touching it, or sense the calm of the ocean without stepping into the water, so too can we receive the healing energy of plants and mushrooms by simply being in their presence.

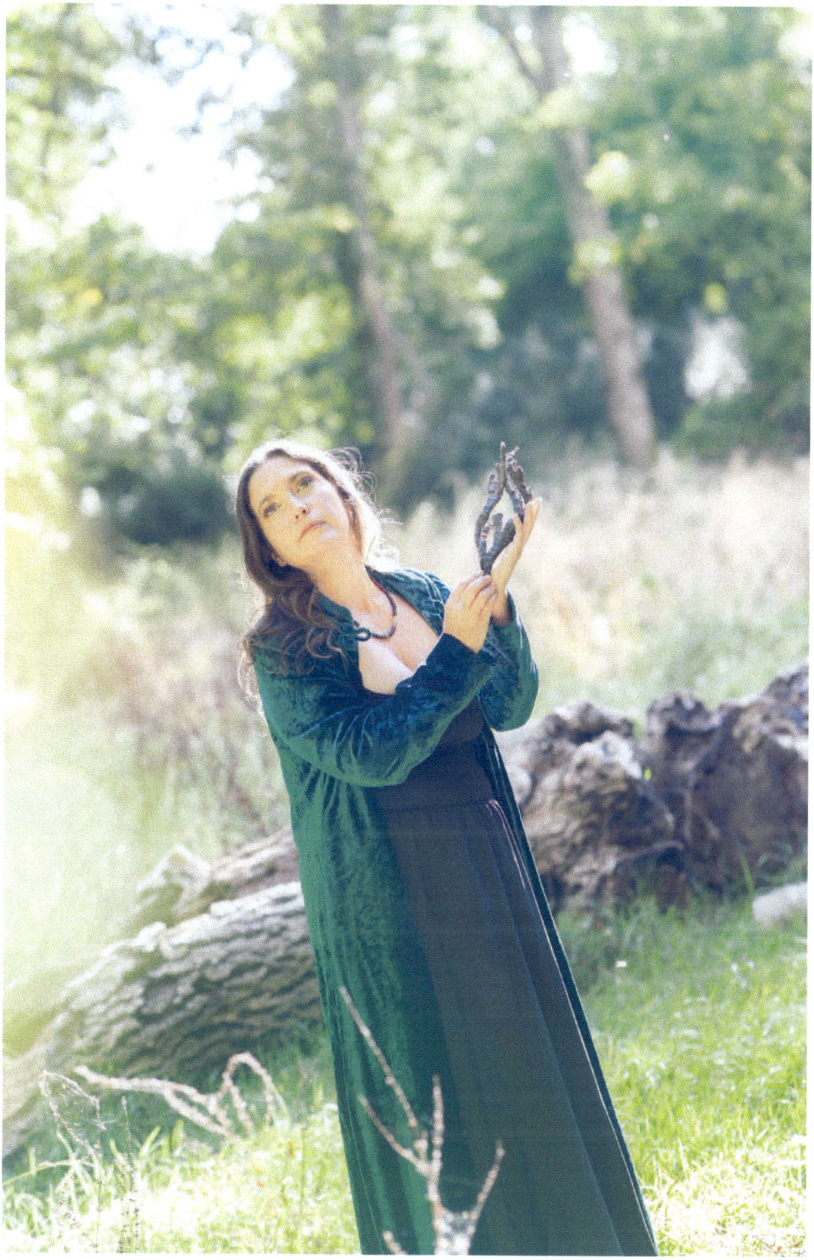

Anecdotal Evidence

Beyond the realm of clinical studies, reishi has garnered a reputation as a powerful adaptogen - one that helps the body resist stress and maintain balance. Many people report that regular consumption of reishi supplements or tea improves sleep quality, reduces anxiety, increases mental clarity and enhances overall well-being.

Reishi mushroom is used often within traditional medicine systems such as Traditional Chinese Medicine. Many people have shared personal accounts of improved health and well-being after incorporating reishi into their daily routines. One of the most common anecdotes involves its use as a powerful immune booster. People often report fewer colds and infections, especially during colder months, together with an increase in vitality and resilience. Others highlight its calming effects and increased ability to handle stress with regular reishi consumption. This aligns with the traditional belief in reishi as a 'Shen tonic,' supporting mental clarity and emotional balance.

In addition, reishi is frequently mentioned in the context of chronic health issues. Many individuals dealing with conditions such as high blood pressure, liver problems, or autoimmune disorders have reported positive changes after taking reishi, particularly in reducing inflammation and enhancing recovery. Some also share stories of tumour regression and improved cancer outcomes after combining reishi with conventional treatments or working with the medicinal mushrooms and other natural therapies such as diet, bio-resonance and oxygen therapy.

I found this reishi growing on a fence panel by the side of the road

Scientific Research

Immune Modulation and Cancer Support

Reishi mushroom has a long history of use in traditional medicine for enhancing the immune system. A 2003 study showed that reishi extract could enhance the activity of Natural Killer (NK) cells in cancer patients, improving the body's ability to fight tumour cells. This study highlights reishi's role in modulating the immune response, particularly in individuals undergoing cancer treatment.

[Study Reference: Gao, Y., Zhou, S., Jiang, W., Huang, M., & Dai, X. Effects of Ganoderma lucidum polysaccharides on immune function. Journal of Clinical Oncology, 2003]

Cardiovascular Benefits

A study published in the Journal of Ethnopharmacology (2006) found that reishi has a beneficial effect on cardiovascular health by improving blood circulation and lowering blood pressure. The triterpenes found in reishi are believed to reduce LDL cholesterol levels, offering protection against atherosclerosis and heart disease.

[Study Reference: Wu, Y. L., Han, H., & He, H. F. Cardiovascular effects of Ganoderma lucidum: a meta-analysis. Journal of Ethnopharmacology, 2006]

Liver Health and Detoxification

Reishi is also known for its hepatoprotective (liver-protecting) effects. A 2012 study revealed that polysaccharides from reishi mushrooms helped protect liver cells from damage induced by toxic chemicals, thereby improving overall liver function. The study highlighted the mushroom's potential role in supporting detoxification.

[Study Reference: Shi, Y., Feng, H., Wu, Y., Zhou, L., & Liu, S. The hepatoprotective effects of Ganoderma lucidum polysaccharides. Phytotherapy Research, 2012]

Anti-inflammatory and Antioxidant Effects

A 2014 study demonstrated that the polysaccharides and triterpenes found in reishi have significant anti-inflammatory and antioxidant properties. These compounds were shown to reduce inflammation in a variety of conditions, from arthritis to inflammatory bowel disease.

[Study Reference: Zhu, X., Wang, Z., Zhou, H., Chen, H., & Tan, J. The anti-inflammatory and antioxidant effects of Ganoderma lucidum. International Journal of Medicinal Mushrooms, 2014]

Mental Health and Fatigue Reduction

A 2017 randomised clinical trial showed that reishi supplementation improved quality of life in individuals suffering from chronic fatigue syndrome. Participants reported reduced levels of fatigue, improved mood, and enhanced overall well-being. Reishi's adaptogenic properties are believed to balance the body's response to stress, making it a popular remedy for combating burnout.

[Study Reference: Kuo, M. C., Chang, C. Y., Tsai, W. J., & Yang, H. P. The adaptogenic effect of Ganoderma lucidum on chronic fatigue. Complementary Therapies in Medicine, 2017]

A Client's Story

Steve is a workman who came to my home to do some repairs. Seeing that I run a healing centre, he opened up about his 15-year-old daughters struggle with mental health. Her anxiety was so severe she was hardly able to leave her room and had stopped attending school. Feeling for the plight of this family, I gave him a combination of reishi, CBD and cacao for her to try.

A week later he called and said he'd started to see changes within her and asked to buy "the biggest tin you've got." He messaged 3 weeks later to say, "thank you! We have our daughter back." She had returned to school and her anxiety had all but disappeared.

How To Use

Use as a tea, tincture or powdered extract on its own or as part of a mushroom blend. Steep dried reishi slices or powder in hot water for 30-45 minutes. It can be taken in the evening to promote calm and improve sleep.

There are many types of reishi – this is Ganoderma applanatum

Featured Recipe - Reishi Hot Chocolate

Ingredients:

- 1 cup almond milk (or any plant-based milk of choice)
- 1 tbsp raw cacao powder (or cocoa powder)
- 1/2 tsp reishi mushroom powder
- 1-2 tsp maple syrup (or coconut sugar)
- 1/4 tsp cinnamon (optional)
- 1/4 tsp vanilla extract (optional)
- Pinch of sea salt (optional, to enhance the flavours)
- 1 tsp coconut oil or cacao butter (optional, for creaminess)

Instructions:

1. **Heat the Milk:** In a small saucepan, gently warm the plant milk over medium heat. Avoid boiling it to preserve the nutrients.
2. **Mix the Dry Ingredients:** In a separate bowl, combine the cacao powder, reishi mushroom powder, cinnamon, and sea salt.
3. **Whisk into the Milk:** Once the milk is warm, slowly whisk in the dry ingredients, ensuring there are no lumps.
4. **Add Sweetener and Vanilla:** Stir in the maple syrup and vanilla extract. Adjust sweetness to taste.
5. **Blend for Creaminess (Optional):** For an extra creamy texture, pour the mixture into a blender, add the coconut oil or cacao butter, and blend for about 20-30 seconds until frothy.
6. **Serve:** Pour the reishi hot chocolate into your favourite mug and enjoy the relaxing and nourishing effects of this soothing drink.

You can garnish it with a sprinkle of cinnamon or cacao powder on top if you like. This is a perfect blend to help unwind and support your immune system at the same time!

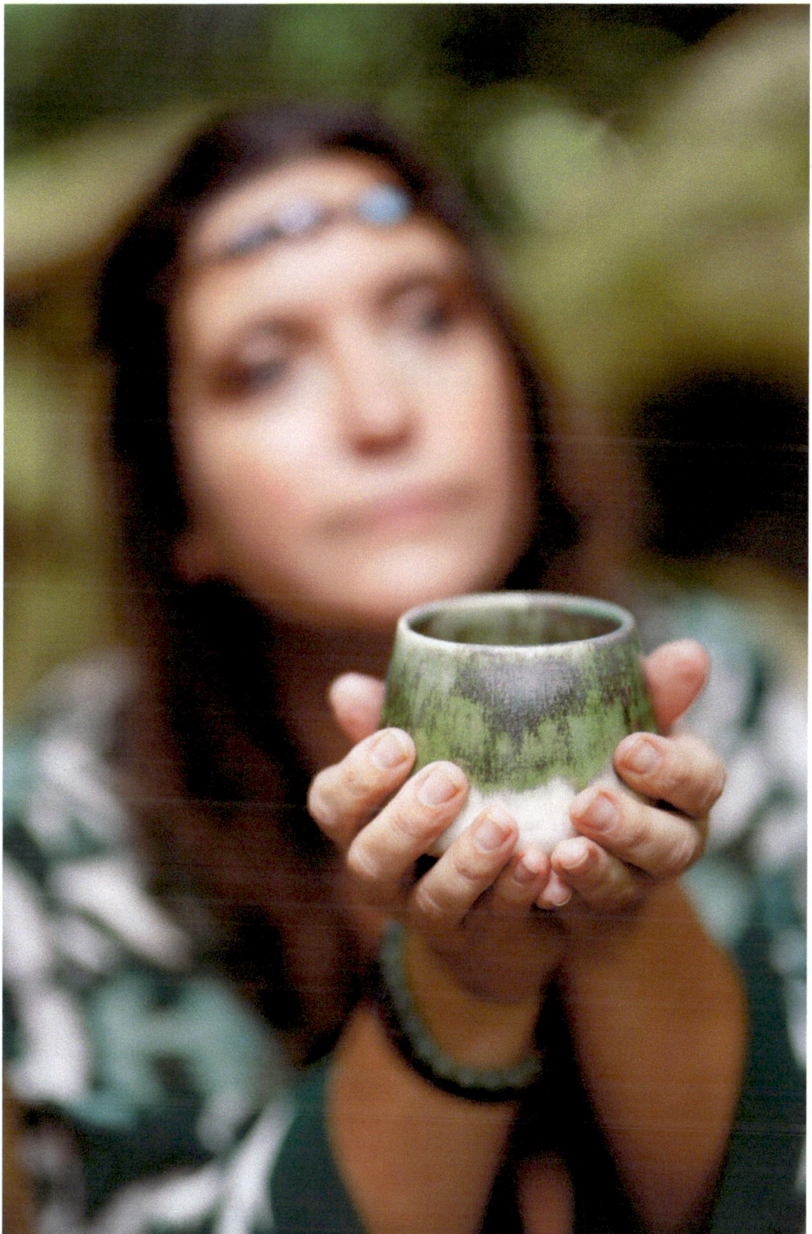

Lion's Mane
– The Brain Mushroom

Other names – *bearded tooth fungus, bearded hedgehog, Hou Tou Gu (monkey head mushroom), pompom mushroom, Yamabushitake (Japanese), natures nutrient for the neurons.*

Botanical – *Hericium erinaceus*

As the name suggests lion's mane looks like a lion's mane! The flesh is white to cream becoming yellow and cloud-like in appearance with teeth up to 6cm long. It grows on hardwood trees, in temperate and sometimes sub-tropical regions throughout the northern hemisphere between June and October, often on dead beech trees. It is a delicious culinary mushroom. In the UK, it is on the "red list" of endangered species and is not permitted to be picked in the wild. However, many producers grow the mushroom for sale.

Historical Use

Lion's mane has been used as a food and in traditional medicine for thousands of years. The earliest written reference is from 618 AD in the Tang Dynasty, China, where it was believed to promote longevity and enhance brain function.

Ancient Chinese herbalists revered lion's mane as a superior medicinal mushroom, which they classified among the "superior herbs" capable of promoting longevity and overall well-being. It was believed to nourish the five internal organs—the liver, spleen, lungs, heart, and kidneys - enhancing overall health and vitality.

While lion's mane has been traditionally used for centuries, its potential as a neuroprotective and brain-boosting agent gained renewed attention in the 20th century. Japanese researcher Dr. Kawagishi was one of the first to isolate compounds known as hericenones and erinacines in the mushroom, which showed promising effects on nerve growth factor (NGF), a protein crucial for the growth and maintenance of neurons.

This discovery catalysed modern research into lion's mane's effects on cognitive health, memory enhancement, and neurodegenerative diseases like Alzheimer's and Parkinson's. Studies have also validated its traditional uses in immune modulation, digestive health, and anti-inflammatory support.

Folklore & Mythology

In Japan, lion's mane is called "Yamabushitake," which translates to "Mountain Priest Mushroom." The name is tied to the Yamabushi monks, ascetic mountain practitioners known for their deep spiritual practices and connection with nature. The Yamabushi monks believed the mushroom held spiritual power, which could be harnessed to enhance meditation, deepen wisdom, and connect with the spiritual realm.

According to legend, the Yamabushi would consume lion's mane to gain spiritual strength and heightened awareness. They believed that the mushroom's energy was linked to the ancient spirits of the mountains, giving those who consumed it the power to connect with nature and the universe.

In Chinese folklore, lion's mane is sometimes associated with forest spirits and mountain deities. It was believed to be a gift from the forest gods, who planted it in the woods as a medicine for both physical and spiritual ailments. Finding a lion's mane mushroom in the wild was considered a sign of good fortune and divine favour, indicating that the person was blessed and protected by the spirits.

There are stories of travellers and hermits who, upon finding lion's mane, experienced visions or prophetic dreams after consuming it. These dreams often contained messages or guidance from the spirits of nature, helping them find their path or gain insight into life's mysteries.

In Buddhist lore, lion's mane is sometimes linked to the Bodhi tree, under which the Buddha attained enlightenment. It is believed that monks who consumed this mushroom experienced enhanced meditation and clarity, helping them on their spiritual path to wisdom.

Some myths tell of a moon goddess who gifted lion's mane to humanity as a remedy for the ills of the mind and body. According to these stories, the moon goddess saw that people were suffering from forgetfulness and confusion, which disconnected them from their spiritual essence. She then planted lion's mane in the deepest forests and high mountain ranges so that those who sought its power could heal and regain clarity.

In these myths, the mushroom was not only seen as a physical remedy but also as a spiritual enhancer, enabling people to reconnect with their soul's true purpose. Those who consumed lion's mane under the light of a full moon were said to receive special blessings, gaining insights into their past lives or connecting with ancestral spirits.

In some Chinese legends, lion's mane is tied to a mythical white lion that roamed the forests of ancient China. This lion, said to be an immortal guardian of knowledge, would leave traces of its mane on trees and logs in the form of lion's mane mushrooms. Those who found and consumed the mushrooms were believed to inherit the lion's wisdom, gaining the ability to communicate with animals, interpret dreams, and see into the future.

This legend emphasizes the transformative power of lion's mane, suggesting that it not only offers physical healing but also grants one the ability to see beyond ordinary perception, opening a pathway to mystical experiences and spiritual understanding.

Healing Properties

Supports cognitive function, heals nerve damage, hormone health, menopausal support, antibacterial, antimicrobial, antioxidant properties, anti-inflammatory, supports health of those with Parkinson's, MS and Alzheimer's and mood regulation.

My Story with Lion's Mane

My personal journey with lion's mane mushroom began with an almost electric realisation. When I first learned about lion's mane, it felt like bells were ringing in my head. As a young girl, my mother suffered from MS, and healing her became part of my life's mission. Sadly, I couldn't achieve this and she died when I was 21. Following her passing, and with her as an inspiration, my mission expanded into the healing practice I run today. Over many decades I have researched looking at ways to support people with MS through nutrition, and I've had the privilege of helping many people successfully. It was when I discovered lion's mane, I thought of how it might benefit those with MS. The excitement of being able to include this powerful mushroom in my work was overwhelming, and its benefits have been nothing short of amazing.

I vividly remember the first time I saw fresh lion's mane mushroom at a farmer's market. After using it as a dried supplement for some time, I was so excited to finally see it in the flesh! A big part of my work is about forming a deep connection with the essence of the plants and mushrooms I use and recommend. Holding the fresh lion's mane, I felt an almost electric charge in my brain. It was as though it was helping all my synapses fire more efficiently - just by holding it! Then, when I brought it home and prepared it, the taste was beyond anything I had imagined - a true culinary delight. Serving fresh lion's mane at my retreats has always been a magical experience, with people constantly amazed by its unique flavour and texture. This mushroom has become a staple in both my nutritional work and the food experiences I offer, embodying not just healing, but connection and discovery.

Anecdotal Evidence

In Chinese Medicine, lion's mane is considered a tonic for the spleen and digestive system, and bestows the courage and prowess of a lion. Lion's mane is often used for its cognitive-enhancing effects. Many individuals claim that regular consumption of lion's mane in powdered form or as an extract has helped them achieve sharper focus, better memory retention, and clearer thinking. This links to traditional use in Asia, where lion's mane has been regarded as a brain tonic. People with conditions such as mild cognitive impairment or ADHD have shared stories of increased mental clarity and improved task performance after including lion's mane into their diets. I remember when my brother first took my mushroom tincture before a business meeting and said, "Wow! That's the first time in my life, I have been able to focus so clearly on one thing."

Additionally, people frequently report feeling more emotionally balanced and less anxious, which they put down to lion's mane's ability to promote the growth of new neural pathways. Those dealing with nerve damage or neurodegenerative diseases, such as MS or Parkinson's, have shared powerful testimonials of improved motor function and reduced symptoms including shaking, brain fog and fatigue.

Scientific Research

<u>Cognitive Function and Neurogenesis</u>
Lion's mane has been extensively studied for its neuroprotective properties. A study conducted in 2009 found that participants who consumed lion's mane extract showed significant improvements in cognitive function compared to the placebo group. This study suggests that compounds in lion's mane stimulate the production of Nerve

Growth Factor (NGF), which plays a crucial role in the growth and survival of neurons. NGF is critical in maintaining cognitive function, especially in aging brains.

[Study Reference: Mori K, Inatomi S, Ouchi K, Azumi Y, Tuchida T. Improving cognitive function with lion's mane in a randomized, placebo-controlled study. Phytotherapy Research, 2009]

Alzheimer's and Dementia Prevention
A 2016 study demonstrated that lion's mane could potentially be used to mitigate Alzheimer's disease progression. The study showed that extracts from lion's mane may help protect brain cells from damage caused by beta-amyloid, a substance linked to Alzheimer's disease. This suggests that lion's mane could support brain health and reduce the risk of cognitive decline as well as delaying neurodegenerative diseases.

[Study Reference: Tzeng, C. P., Cheng, C. Y., Lee, L. Y., Li, H. H., & Wu, Y. P. Neuroprotective effects of Hericium erinaceus mycelium in Alzheimer's disease model. Journal of Functional Foods, 2016]

Anxiety and Depression Reduction
Lion's mane has been found to have antidepressant and anti-anxiety properties. A 2010 study indicated that consumption of lion's mane cookies reduced symptoms of depression and anxiety in a group of women over four weeks. The study attributes these effects to the mushroom's ability to modulate inflammation and neurogenesis in the brain.

[Study Reference: Nagano, M., Shimizu, K., Kondo, R., Hayashi, C., Sato, D., & Kitagawa, Y. Reduction of depression and anxiety with lion's mane mushroom. Biomedical Research, 2010]

Nerve Repair and Myelination

Research published in 2014 found that lion's mane can stimulate nerve regeneration after injury. Rats with peripheral nerve injury treated with lion's mane extract showed faster recovery of motor function. This study suggests that lion's mane promotes the synthesis of myelin, the protective sheath surrounding nerves, improving nerve repair.

[Study Reference: Wong, K. H., Sabaratnam, V., Abdullah, N., Kuppusamy, U. R., & Naidu, M. Potential nerve regenerative properties of Hericium erinaceus. International Journal of Medicinal Mushrooms, 2014]

Antioxidant and Anti-inflammatory Properties

Lion's mane contains high levels of antioxidants, which are essential for reducing oxidative stress in the body. A 2017 study published in the International Journal of Medicinal Mushrooms showed that lion's mane extracts reduced markers of inflammation and oxidative stress in animal models. These findings suggest that lion's mane could potentially support overall brain and cardiovascular health.

[Study Reference: Li, W., Chen, W., Feng, J., Wang, Y., & Cao, W. The anti-inflammatory and antioxidant effects of Hericium erinaceus extract. International Journal of Medicinal Mushrooms, 2017]

A Client's Story

Brian came to see me for a consultation following a brain injury resulting from a car accident that had left him severely injured. He was partially paralysed with impaired cognitive function affecting his memory and speech. After the consult, I recommended that he take a variety of supplements including lion's mane as part of a mushroom blend. 6 weeks later his mobility and brain recall improved significantly. After 3 months he was able to return to work, something he feared he may never be able to do again.

How To Use

Lion's mane can be eaten either fresh or dried as a culinary mushroom. It can be eaten raw – however, this can cause digestive discomfort to some, so it is recommended to be cooked – either fried, baked or added to soups and stews. It is sometimes used as a substitute for meat and fish due to its fleshy, nutritionally dense make-up.

You can take a lion's mane extract as a tincture, powder or pill – on its own or as part of a mushroom complex. It is best used as an extract powder in smoothies, coffee, or tea. Regular use is recommended.

Featured Recipe - Lion's Mane Steak

Ingredients:

- 2 large lion's mane mushroom caps (cleaned and trimmed)
- 3 tbsp tamari (or soy sauce)
- 1 tbsp fresh ginger, finely grated
- 2 cloves garlic, minced
- 1 red chili, finely chopped (adjust based on heat preference)
- 1 tbsp sesame oil (or olive oil)
- 1 tbsp maple syrup (for a touch of sweetness)
- 1 tsp toasted sesame seeds (optional, for garnish)
- 1 spring onion, chopped (optional, for garnish)

Instructions:

1. **Prepare the Marinade:** In a small bowl, mix together the tamari, grated ginger, minced garlic, chopped chilli, sesame oil, rice vinegar and maple syrup.
2. **Marinate the lion's mane:** Place the lion's mane mushroom caps in a shallow dish and pour the marinade over them.

Ensure that the mushrooms are evenly coated. Let them marinate for at least 30 minutes, turning occasionally for an even soak. For a deeper flavour, you can let them marinate for up to 2 hours in the fridge.

3. **Cook the Mushrooms:**
    - **Grill Method:** Preheat your grill or a grill pan over medium heat. Once hot, place the marinated lion's mane caps on the grill and cook for about 4-5 minutes on each side, until golden brown and slightly crispy on the edges.
    - **Pan Method:** Heat a pan over medium heat with a little oil. Once hot, add the marinated lion's mane mushrooms and cook for about 4-5 minutes per side, until browned and cooked through. You can spoon some of the leftover marinade over the mushrooms as they cook for extra flavour.
4. **Garnish and Serve:** Once the lion's mane steaks are cooked, remove them from the heat and let them rest for a minute. Sprinkle with toasted sesame seeds and chopped spring onions, if desired.
5. **Serve and Enjoy:** Serve your lion's mane steaks with a side of steamed vegetables, rice, or salad for a satisfying and hearty meal.

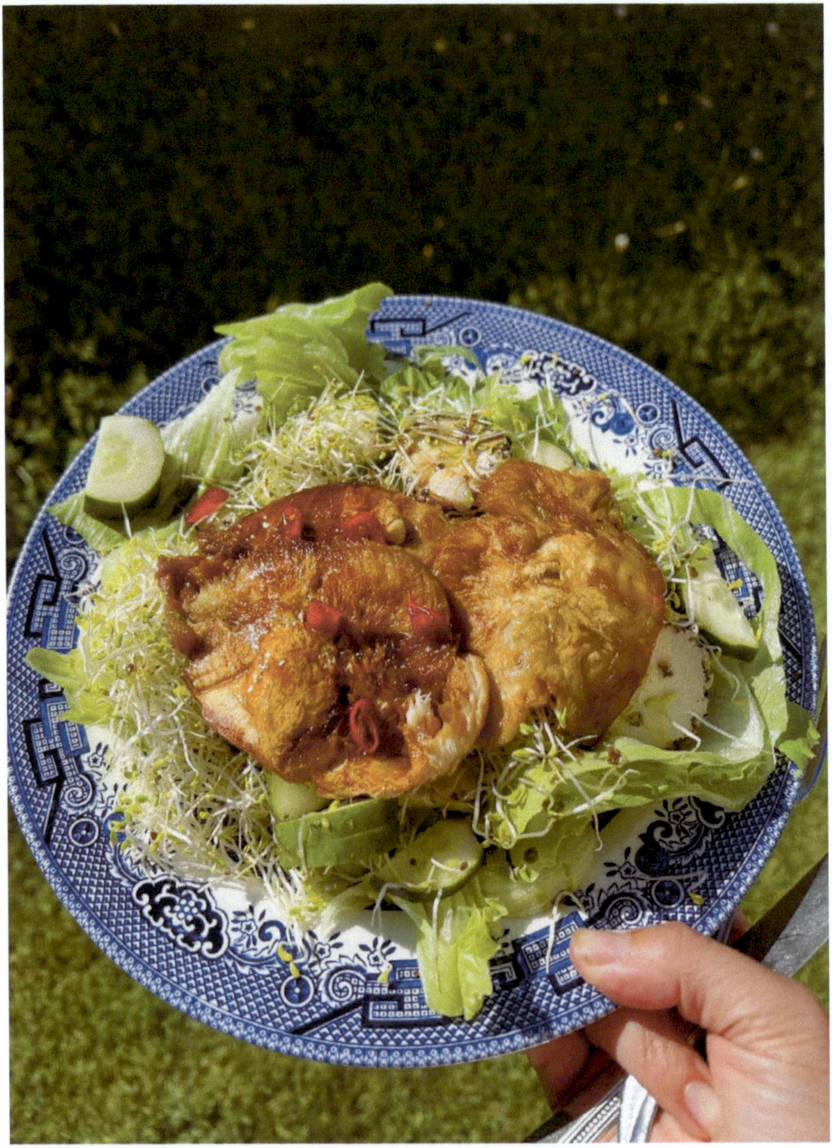

Turkey Tail
– The Mushroom by the Riverbank

Other names – *Yun Zhi (Cloud Mushroom - Chinese), Kawaratake (Mushroom by the Riverbank – Japanese), rainbow bridge mushroom.*

Botanical – *Trametes versicolor*

As the common name suggests, this mushroom resembles the fan-like tail of a miniature turkey. They are found growing most often on deciduous dead wood on the forest floor, 2-8cm across, although they have been found on living trees and on occasion on conifers, which is rare for mushrooms. They grow in clusters and can be a variety of colours – brown & grey are most common – its identification is helped by its white outer ring. Turkey tail is inedible, and needs to be processed to consume it.

Historical Use

In Southeast Asia, turkey tail had been used to make decoctions for various health issues since the 2nd century BC.

In various cultures, turkey tail was not only a medicinal mushroom but also a symbol of a healthy, thriving ecosystem. Its presence on decaying logs and trees was seen as a sign of regeneration, indicating that the forest was in balance. For indigenous and ancient peoples, mushrooms like turkey tail were considered messengers of nature, demonstrating the interconnectedness of life, death, and rebirth in the natural world.

Collecting turkey tail was often done with ceremonial respect, acknowledging its role as a teacher of cycles and an indicator of ecological health.

Native American tribes also have a long history of using turkey tail for its healing properties. This mushroom was traditionally boiled into teas to treat respiratory illnesses, colds, and infections. Turkey tail was considered a powerful remedy for lung issues due to its supportive and immune-boosting qualities.

In Siberian shamanic traditions, turkey tail has been used as a spiritual and physical protector. Shamans viewed it as a guardian mushroom that could protect against negative energy and enhance one's spiritual strength. It was often burned as an incense or infused into rituals to purify and cleanse both the body and the spirit.

The mushroom was also believed to carry the energy of the forest, acting as a bridge between humans and the natural world. By using turkey tail, shamans aimed to connect with the spirits of nature, seeking guidance and protection.

In the 1970s, researchers in Japan developed PSK, an extract derived from turkey tail, which became a clinically approved treatment for cancer in Japan, particularly as a complementary therapy alongside chemotherapy and radiation.

In China, researchers isolated PSP (Polysaccharopeptide) from turkey tail, which showed similar immune-boosting and cancer-fighting properties. Both PSK and PSP continue to be studied and utilised in contemporary medicine, blending ancient herbal knowledge with modern science.

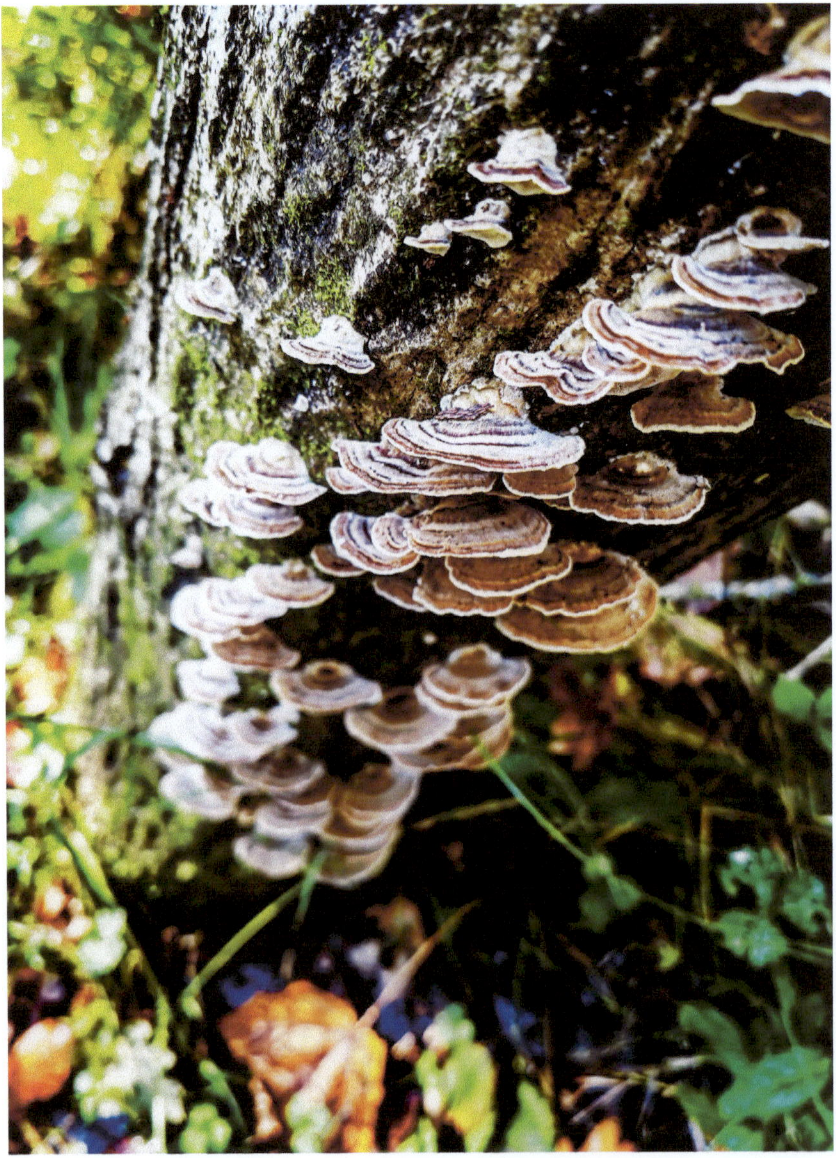

Folklore & Mythology

In some Chinese legends, turkey tail is associated with the mythical Phoenix, a bird symbolising immortality, rebirth, and renewal. The mushroom's colourful, fan-like shape was thought to resemble the feathers of the Phoenix, and it was believed that turkey tail was a gift left behind by the Phoenix to bestow health, protection, and transformation upon the forest and its inhabitants.

The mushroom was not only a symbol of resilience but also a marker of divine presence. According to these stories, finding turkey tail was seen as a blessing from the Phoenix, ensuring that those who discovered it would receive protection and vitality.

In Native American traditions, turkey tail was considered a healing spirit of the forest. Tribes viewed the mushroom as a powerful protector and believed that its energy could absorb and neutralise illness. Medicine men and women would brew turkey tail into teas and use it in healing ceremonies, calling upon the mushroom's spirit to cleanse the body and restore balance.

Turkey tail was also believed to be a guide for the lost. When people found themselves disoriented in the forest, they would look for the mushroom as a sign that they were not alone and that they were being watched over by the spirits of the land. In some legends, the mushroom's appearance was seen as a message from ancestors, guiding individuals toward safety or spiritual enlightenment.

In various myths, turkey tail's colourful bands were seen as sacred symbols. Each band was thought to represent different elements or energies of the natural world, such as earth, water, fire, air, and spirit. This gave the mushroom a protective and balancing quality, as it embodied the harmonious coexistence of all these elements.

Some ancient stories say that the colours of turkey tail were painted by the spirits as a reminder of nature's beauty, and the incredible interconnectedness of all life. In these tales, turkey tail was a sacred, living mandala, showing that everything in nature is interconnected and unified. People believed that meditating on the mushroom's patterns or using it in rituals could help them align their own energies with the natural world, achieving harmony and peace.

In shamanic and indigenous traditions across various cultures, turkey tail is sometimes referred to as the "Rainbow Bridge Mushroom." It was believed that its bands of colour reflected the pathway between the physical world and the spirit world. Shamans would use the mushroom in ceremonies to guide souls on their journey, ensuring safe passage between realms.

In Siberian folklore, turkey tail was also seen as a protector of the forest's energy, and shamans believed it helped maintain the balance between human activity and natural processes. When forests were over-harvested or mistreated, turkey tail's appearance was thought to be a warning from the spirits to respect and restore balance to the land.

Healing Properties

Immune system support, antiviral, antioxidant-rich, gut health support, anti-inflammatory, cancer support, immune modulation, antibacterial, liver detoxification, respiratory health and increasing microbiome diversity.

My Story with Turkey Tail

I remember walking through the woods, marvelling at the sight of turkey tail mushrooms fanning across a fallen log. Their soft, velvety texture and beautiful, frilled edges brought a smile to my face, even before I knew about their medicinal power. It's incredible how nature places such potent remedies right in front of us, but we often overlook them. That sense of awe only deepened when I learned about the health benefits of this remarkable mushroom.

Collecting turkey tail mushrooms with my children became a regular adventure, turning walks into rewarding foraging experiences. The ease of identifying them made it all the more fun, and making teas and tinctures from our harvests became a joyful ritual.

One of my favourite combinations is turkey tail with goji berries made into a tea – it is a pairing that goes together superbly. The real magic, though, is sharing the connection of the earth with my children and friends, spreading the knowledge that so much of what we need is right there, waiting for us – when we have eyes to see, and the drive to look for them.

Anecdotal evidence

Turkey tail mushrooms have earned a significant place in the realm of immune-supporting natural remedies, with many people sharing stories of its ability to help them overcome persistent infections and support recovery from chronic illnesses. Cancer patients in particular often cite turkey tail as something that has helped increase energy levels and improved responses to conventional treatments. This has now been studied in Japan and is used alongside conventional cancer treatments. Many people turn to turkey tail to manage or prevent colds and flu, reporting that regular consumption of turkey tail tea or tinctures dramatically reduces the frequency and severity of illnesses.

There are also anecdotal reports of turkey tail aiding gut health, with people stating they got relief from conditions like IBS and general digestive discomfort. Its ease of identification and availability in nature has made it a favourite among foragers, who often describe the joy of brewing fresh turkey tail tea as a healing ritual. Many people appreciate its gentle but noticeable effects on their immune system, describing a general sense of wellbeing and resilience.

Scientific Research

Immune System Support
Turkey tail is renowned for its immune-boosting properties. A 2012 study published in the Journal of Clinical Oncology demonstrated that turkey tail extract (PSK) significantly improved the immune function of women undergoing chemotherapy for breast cancer. PSK increased the activity of NK cells, T-cells, and other immune cells, helping the body fight cancer.

[Study Reference: Standish, L. J., Wenner, C. A., Sweet, E. S., Martzen, M. R., & Novack, J. turkey tail extract enhances immune response in cancer patients. Journal of Clinical Oncology, 2012]

Gut Health and Microbiome Support
A 2015 study found that turkey tail contains prebiotic fibres that nourish beneficial gut bacteria. The study showed that turkey tail extracts improved gut health by promoting the growth of Lactobacillus and Bifidobacterium, beneficial bacteria associated with enhanced digestion and immune function.

[Study Reference: Harikrishnan, R., Kim, M. C., & Balasundaram, C. Prebiotic effects of turkey tail polysaccharides. International Journal of Medicinal Mushrooms, 2015]

Anticancer Properties
Turkey tail is known for its potent anticancer properties. A 2016 study published in Cancer Immunology Research showed that turkey tail polysaccharides inhibit tumour growth in animal models. The study highlighted the mushroom's potential as an adjunct therapy for cancer, particularly for its ability to enhance the efficacy of conventional treatments.

[Study Reference: Smith, J. E., Rowan, N. J., & Sullivan, R. turkey tail

polysaccharides and their anticancer properties. Cancer Immunology Research, 2016]

Anti-inflammatory and Antioxidant Effects
A 2018 study examined the anti-inflammatory and antioxidant effects of turkey tail. Researchers found that the mushroom's polysaccharides and phenolic compounds significantly reduced oxidative stress and inflammation in animal models, suggesting potential benefits for conditions like arthritis and heart disease.

[Study Reference: Lull, C., Wichers, H. J., & Savelkoul, H. F. Anti-inflammatory effects of Trametes versicolor. International Journal of Medicinal Mushrooms, 2018]

Respiratory Health and Immune Defence
Turkey tail has long been used to support respiratory health. A 2019 study found that turkey tail extract improved lung function and reduced symptoms in patients with chronic obstructive pulmonary disease (COPD). The study highlighted the mushroom's ability to modulate immune responses, making it beneficial for those with compromised respiratory systems.

[Study Reference: Chen, H., Li, Z., & Zhang, X. turkey tail extract for respiratory health. Journal of Ethnopharmacology, 2019]

A Client's Story

Colin is a senior manager at a multi-national company who had developed MS, and came to see me for a consultation. He wanted to be active for his young daughter and his job but was struggling with daily tasks. He used a combination of turkey tail, lion's mane and reishi alongside a profound detoxification programme and dietary changes alongside other supplements.

Within 3 months he was noticeably better, and now he is in complete remission from the symptoms of MS.

How To Use

Brew into tea or make tinctures. Simmer dried mushrooms or powder for at least 30 minutes to release their medicinal properties.

Featured Recipe - Turkey Tail & Goji Berry Tea

Ingredients:

- 1-2 small handfuls of dried turkey tail mushrooms (or 1-2 tsp turkey tail powder)
- 1 tbsp dried goji berries
- 4 cups of water
- 1 cinnamon stick (optional, for added warmth)
- 1-2 slices of fresh ginger (optional, for a spicy kick)
- 1-2 tsp maple syrup (optional, for sweetness)

Instructions:

1. **Prepare the turkey tail:** If using dried turkey tail mushrooms, rinse them under cold water to remove any debris. If using turkey tail powder, you can skip this step.
2. **Simmer the Mushrooms:** In a medium saucepan, bring the 4 cups of water to a boil. Once boiling, reduce the heat to low, add the turkey tail mushrooms (or powder), and let them simmer for 30-60 minutes. The longer you simmer, the more potent the tea will be. If you're using powder, 30 minutes should be sufficient.
3. **Add Goji Berries:** About 10 minutes before the simmering time is up, add the dried goji berries to the pot. If using cinnamon or ginger, add them at this time as well.
4. **Strain the Tea:** After simmering, strain the tea into a teapot or mug, removing the turkey tail mushrooms and any added spices.
5. **Sweeten (Optional):** Stir in maple syrup if you prefer a touch of sweetness.

6. **Serve and Enjoy:** Pour the tea into your favourite cup and enjoy it warm. The tea will have a rich, earthy flavour from the turkey tail, complemented by the natural sweetness of the goji berries.

This tea is not only delicious but also an excellent way to support your immune system, with the incredible health benefits of the combination of turkey tail and goji berries.

Cordyceps
– The Energiser Mushroom

Other names – Viagra of the Himalayas, *Zombie ant fungus, winter worm, Tochukaso (Japanese), Yartsa gunbu (Tibetan – Summer grass, winter worm).*

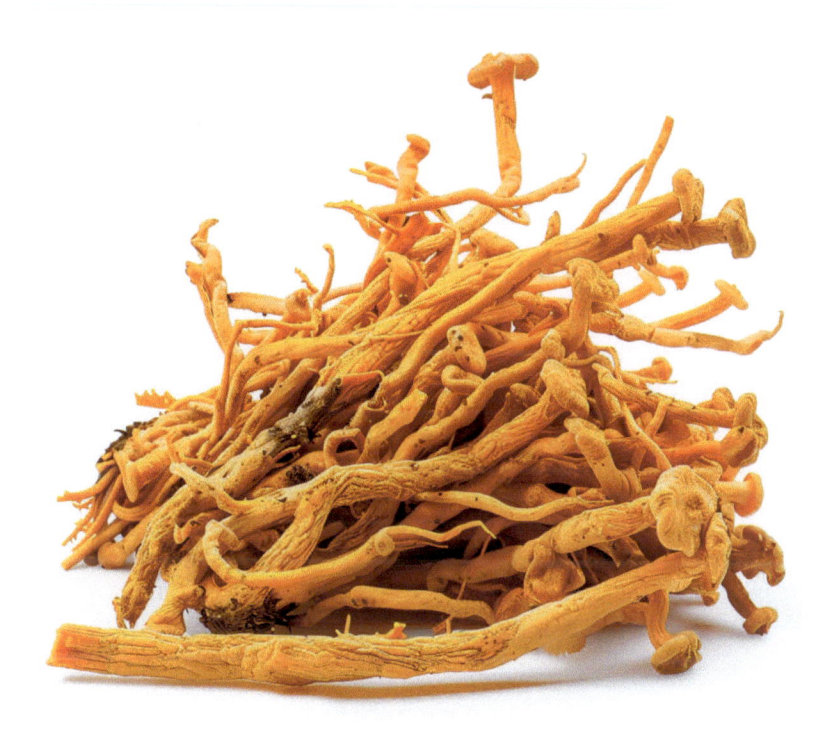

Botanical – *Cordyceps species*

When grown in nature, cordyceps can look like a dark, thick grass. It grows up to 10cm long and takes 4-6 weeks to complete a growing cycle. It is extremely hard to find in the wild and is mainly cultivated for sale, which results in different coloured specimens. The main variety is Cordyceps sinensis, which is thought to be a parasitic mushroom that grows on caterpillars, moths and dragonfly larvae. However, it has been observed that cordyceps actually supports the life of their hosts, in sometimes harsh environments, and only appear once the host has died. The evolving and deepening understanding of this relationship shows the symbiosis of nature.

There are over 350 different species of cordyceps found worldwide, and they can grow on a variety of mediums. However, since 1964, Cordyceps sinensis has been recorded officially as a herbal drug in Chinese pharmacopoeia. Cordyceps sinensis is grown on grain-based substrate, often from mushroom bio-mass technology, so vegans do not need to be concerned with consuming this mushroom.

Historical Use

Cordyceps has been used for at least hundreds of years and possibly much longer in China, Tibet and other places at high elevated plateaus. The first time it appears in writing is in 1694 in the Chinese Materia Medica book *Ben Cao Bei Yao* by scholar Wang Ang (still in print today). The mushroom has been used to treat fatigue, coughs, sexual impotency and kidney problems.

In Tibetan medicine, cordyceps mushrooms were incorporated into traditional formulas for treating various conditions, including weakness, lung diseases, and energy depletion. They were often mixed with other herbs and animal products to create powerful tonics believed to restore balance and harmony within the body.

Tibetan monks, particularly those practising in high altitudes, valued cordyceps for its ability to enhance physical stamina and endurance, helping them maintain rigorous spiritual practices and meditation sessions in the harsh, oxygen-deprived mountain environments. The mushroom was believed to strengthen both body and spirit, promoting a sense of balance and resilience necessary for spiritual growth.

Folklore & Mythology

As mentioned above in Tibetan culture, Cordyceps is known as "Yartsa Gunbu," meaning "Summer Grass, Winter Worm." The mythology that surrounds this is that it was believed that mountain deities blessed the land with Yartsa Gunbu as a way to provide strength and resilience to the people living in the harsh high-altitude environments. Consuming the fungus was thought to imbue the spirit of the mountains, giving those who consumed it the stamina and vitality needed to survive and thrive in these extreme conditions.

A popular Tibetan legend tells the story of the Snow Lion, a mythical creature believed to reside in the snowy peaks of the Himalayas. The Snow Lion, a symbol of strength, purity, and courage, was said to have a special connection with cordyceps. According to the legend, the Snow Lion would roam the highlands, and wherever its breath touched the earth, cordyceps would grow, sprouting from the bodies of caterpillars.

This was seen as a blessing from the Snow Lion, offering a gift that could revitalise and heal. It was believed that consuming cordyceps allowed people to channel the strength and courage of the Snow Lion, helping them face life's challenges with vigour and resilience.

The unique parasitic nature of cordyceps, which involves transforming from an insect to a mushroom-like structure, inspired stories about its transformative powers. In Chinese folklore, it was believed that cordyceps held the essence of transformation, making it a sacred tool for alchemy and spiritual growth.

Some ancient tales suggest that cordyceps could transform weakness into strength, symbolizing the belief that nature has the power to turn even the most vulnerable state (a dying caterpillar) into a source of life-giving energy. This transformative power was thought to not only affect the body but also the spirit, granting those who consumed it a chance to elevate their spiritual state and achieve a deeper connection with the universe.

In some Chinese legends, cordyceps is associated with the Sky Dragon, a mythical being responsible for controlling the weather and protecting the land. It was said that when the Sky Dragon exhaled its breath over the mountains, it would infuse the caterpillars with its energy, causing cordyceps to grow. The fungus was thus seen as a manifestation of the Sky Dragon's power, holding within it the energy of the heavens and the mountains.

Consuming cordyceps was believed to grant the strength and vitality of the Sky Dragon, helping warriors and athletes enhance their physical abilities. Those who consumed it with reverence and gratitude were thought to receive the dragon's blessings, ensuring strength in battle, longevity, and protection against misfortune.

Healing Properties

Infertility, athletic and sexual performance, endurance, recovery from exertion or illness, anti-viral, helps lungs – asthma & COPD, anti-tumour activity, balances cholesterol, regulates blood sugar and helps kidney health.

My Story with Cordyceps

After delving deeper into the world of medicinal mushrooms, I remember reading about cordyceps for the first time and feeling both fascinated and unsettled. The thought of a mushroom that grows through the brain of its insect host was almost too much to process! I couldn't help but wonder, "Could this happen to humans?" I researched extensively, only to discover, with relief, that cordyceps cannot infect humans like something out of a horror film. In fact, its role in human health is quite the opposite - it supports vitality, energy, and reproductive health - so important in light of rising infertility rates.

Once I was convinced of its vegan nature, and I began using cordyceps, it quickly became my go-to when I needed an extra boost of energy and vitality, especially during demanding times. I also found that combining it with other mushrooms like lion's mane provided incredible synergy - far surpassing the effects of either on its own. This pairing brought together mental clarity and a deep, sustained energy that felt magical. It's a perfect example of how nature's elements can work together to create something greater than the sum of its parts.

Anecdotal Evidence

Cordyceps has gained a powerful reputation in athletic circles for some time. Its use has become so mainstream that you may find people at your local gym taking it to support their workouts, which would be have been virtually unknown 30 years ago. In 1993 the Chinese Women's team achieved unprecedented success at the Beijing

Olympics. They won multiple Gold medals in endurance events as well breaking World records. It is reputed they were using an ancient Chinese formula used to massively enhance athletic performance. Sceptics have suggested the use of additional chemical substances led to these astonishing performances. A health company bought the rights to this formula, removed some of the 'questionable ingredients' and released it – with the main ingredient being cordyceps.

Cordyceps is known for its remarkable energy-boosting properties. Many people rave about cordyceps for enhancing endurance, stamina, and overall performance, both in training, competition (and in the bedroom). Many people report increased physical energy without the jittery side effects associated with stimulants, making cordyceps a favourite among those looking to support their vitality naturally. Those with chronic fatigue or respiratory issues, such as asthma, have shared accounts of improved breathing and better energy management when taking cordyceps regularly.

Cordyceps is also praised for its effects on libido and fertility, with many individuals claiming a noticeable boost in sexual health and vitality. People describe feeling more vital, youthful, and energised after adding cordyceps into their regime, aligning with its traditional use in supporting longevity and reproductive health in Chinese medicine.

Scientific Research

Athletic Performance and Oxygen Utilization
Cordyceps has gained a reputation for improving athletic performance and stamina. A study found that participants who took cordyceps supplements experienced significant improvements in oxygen uptake (VO2 max), a critical factor in endurance. This increase in oxygen efficiency was attributed to cordyceps' ability to boost adenosine triphosphate (ATP) production, the energy currency of the cells.

[Study Reference: Chen, S., Li, Z., Krochmal, R., Abrazado, M., Kim, W., Cooper, C. B. Effects of Cordyceps sinensis on oxygen uptake. Journal of Dietary Supplements, 2014]

Anti-ageing and Longevity
A 2017 study explored cordyceps' anti-aging effects, focusing on its ability to enhance mitochondrial function and combat oxidative stress. Researchers found that cordyceps helped reduce age-related oxidative damage in animal models, contributing to improved energy levels, endurance, and longevity.

[Study Reference: Wang, S., & Shiao, M. Anti-aging properties of Cordyceps sinensis. Journal of Gerontology, 2017]

Immune Function Support
Cordyceps has been shown to modulate the immune system, enhancing its response to infections and diseases. A 2016 study demonstrated that cordyceps supplementation increased the activity of macrophages and NK cells, both essential components of the immune efence system. These results suggest cordyceps may offer immune support, especially in individuals with weakened immunity.

[Study Reference: Zhang, Y., Li, E., & Wang, Z. Immunomodulatory effects of Cordyceps sinensis. Journal of Functional Foods, 2016]

Respiratory Health
Cordyceps has been traditionally used to treat respiratory conditions like asthma and chronic bronchitis. A 2013 study found that cordyceps extract improved lung function in individuals with moderate-to-severe asthma by reducing inflammation and opening up the airways. The findings support cordyceps' use in promoting respiratory health.

[Study Reference: Liu, X., Zheng, P., & Jiang, X. The effects of Cordyceps on asthma. Phytotherapy Research, 2013]

Sexual Health and Libido Enhancement
A 2015 study on male fertility and sexual health revealed that cordyceps supplementation improved sperm count, mobility, and testosterone levels in participants. This study highlights cordyceps' potential in enhancing sexual health and treating infertility issues.

[Study Reference: Wu, Z., Liang, C., & Fang, X. The effects of Cordyceps sinensis on male fertility. Journal of Andrology, 2015

A Client's Story

Penny came to see me for a consultation. It had been 5 years since her third child was born and she still had not regained her sex drive. This was causing problems in her relationship as well as affecting her mental health and confidence. I recommended she take a dual extract mushroom tincture with cordyceps and other mushrooms alongside the potent nutrient-rich superfood shilajit. Within a few weeks I got a message saying her 'bedroom activity' has been better than ever before and she was overjoyed – as was her partner.

How To Use

Take as an extract from a reputable company, as a tincture, powder or pill for energy, stamina, and vitality. You can take on its own or as part of a mushroom complex. Between 1.5g to 4.5g a day is recommended.

Featured Recipe - Cordyceps Superfood Smoothie

A cordyceps superfood smoothie is a great way to boost your energy levels, support endurance, and nourish your body with vital nutrients. Cordyceps is known for its ability to enhance oxygen utilization and stamina, making it a perfect addition to a smoothie for energising.

Here is a super recipe for a cordyceps smoothie that is vegan-friendly, packed with adaptogens and is ideal for sustained energy:

Ingredients:

- **1 tsp cordyceps mushroom powder or a mushroom complex with cordyceps**
- **1 frozen banana** (for creaminess and natural sweetness)
- **1/2 cup frozen berries** (blueberries, raspberries, or mixed berries)
- **1 tbsp raw cacao powder** (for added energy and mood boost)
- **1 tbsp All You Need Superfood Powder** (or similar)
- **1 tbsp chia seeds** (for omega-3s and sustained energy)
- **1 tbsp almond butter** (or any nut butter for healthy fats and protein)
- **1/2 cup almond milk** (or your favourite plant-based milk)
- **1/2 cup coconut water** (for electrolytes and hydration)
- **1 tsp maca powder** (optional, for hormonal balance and energy)
- **1/2 tsp cinnamon** (optional, for blood sugar balance)
- **Ice cubes** (optional, for a chilled and thicker consistency)

Instructions:

1. **Blend**:
    - Add all ingredients to a high-speed blender.

- Blend on high until smooth and creamy. If the consistency is too thick, add more coconut water or almond milk until you reach your desired texture.

2. **Taste and Adjust**:
    - Taste the smoothie and adjust for sweetness or flavour. If you prefer it sweeter, add a few dates or some maple syrup.

3. **Serve**:
    - Pour into your favourite glass or jar and enjoy immediately for freshness and more nutrients.

Liberty Cap
– The Magic Mushroom

Other names – *Magic Mushroom, Shrooms, Hippy's Friend, Cap Hud, Divine Flesh, Little Flowers of the Gods.*

Botanical – *Psilocybe semilanceata*

There are a variety of the Psilocybe mushrooms that grow in different countries around the world. In the UK, *Psilocybe semilanceata* are little mushrooms that grow to about 5cm high. They appear in fields between Sept and Dec. They are whitish with a yellow-brown nipple on the top. They contain the active ingredients psilocybin and psilocin which can cause hallucinations, vomiting and nausea. Other worldwide varieties include the revered *Psilocybe Mexicana*.

Legal Information

In the UK where I live, these mushrooms have been illegal to pick, prepare, eat or sell since 2005 and when dried are considered a class A drug. However due to the growing anecdotal and scientific research on their medicinal benefits, many believe change is coming. Different countries have different legislation. If taking in a country that is legal, do so with utmost care and professional supervision (see How To Use).

Historical Use

Psilocybin mushrooms, often referred to as "magic mushrooms," have a rich history of use in religious, spiritual, and shamanic practices around the world. Ingesting these mushrooms with the psychoactive compound psilocybin has been done for thousands of years by indigenous cultures for its mind-altering effects.

In Mesoamerica, the use of psilocybin mushrooms can be traced back at least 3,000 years. The Aztecs referred to these sacred mushrooms as "teonanácatl," meaning "flesh of the gods," and used them in religious ceremonies to communicate with deities, gain spiritual insight, and predict the future. Spanish chroniclers from the 16th century documented the use of these mushrooms by the Aztecs, noting their central role in religious rituals.

The Mayans also used psilocybin mushrooms in their spiritual practices, as evidenced by mushroom stones and carvings found in Guatemala and Honduras. These artefacts, dating back to 1000 BCE, depict figures holding or wearing mushrooms, suggesting their significance in Mayan culture.

In the 1950s, psilocybin mushrooms gained attention in the Western world when R. Gordon Wasson, an American banker and amateur ethnomycologist, participated in a Mazatec mushroom ceremony in Mexico. Wasson's experiences, documented in *Life* magazine, helped spark the modern psychedelic movement, leading to widespread interest in the potential of psilocybin mushrooms for spiritual exploration and psychological healing.

Interestingly, the name "liberty cap" is also tied to the Phrygian cap, an ancient symbol of freedom that became popular during the French Revolution. This has led to speculation that the mushroom's name reflects its ability to expand consciousness and liberate the mind, breaking free from the constraints of everyday reality.

Folklore & Mythology

Psilocybin mushrooms have a rich mythological and cultural significance, particularly in Mesoamerican cultures where they were revered as sacred tools for communicating with the divine. The Aztecs and other indigenous groups believed that psilocybin mushrooms were a gift from the gods, allowing humans to access higher states of consciousness and spiritual knowledge.

In many cultures, psilocybin mushrooms were considered to have the power to heal both the body and the soul. They were often used in rituals to connect with ancestors, seek guidance, and understand the mysteries of the universe. The indigenous people of Mexico and other countries continue to use psilocybin mushrooms in their spiritual practices. They are consumed during ceremonies to invoke visions and commune with the spirit world.

Some scholars suggest that ancient Greek and Roman myths may have connections to the use of psychedelic mushrooms, including liberty caps. It's believed that the Eleusinian Mysteries, a series of sacred rites performed in ancient Greece, might have included the use of psychoactive substances like psilocybin mushrooms.

In medieval England, mushrooms like the liberty cap were often considered to have magical powers. They were linked to witches and sorcery, with some believing that they were used in potion-making or spell-casting. The association with witches led to some of the negative connotations surrounding mushrooms and psychedelic experiences during this period.

The use of psilocybin mushrooms in spiritual contexts often involves specific rituals and ceremonies designed to create a sacred space for the experience. These practices emphasize respect for the mushroom's power and the importance of setting an intention before consuming the mushrooms.

In the 1960's and 70's, psilocybin mushrooms had become symbols of the counterculture and the psychedelic movement, representing a quest for expanded consciousness and personal liberation. This association has led to both fascination and controversy, as society shifts its perception following the growing awareness of psilocybin use for mental health, spirituality, and personal growth.

My Story with liberty Cap

My first experience with liberty cap mushrooms came during my teenage years when I lived in Florida. An hour after taking the mushrooms I entered another level of reality. It was a profound moment, one that opened my mind to realms of possibility far beyond what society had taught me. I had always been a deep thinker, often questioning the nature of life and our place in the world, and when I encountered these mushrooms, it felt as though everything finally clicked. There was a deep sense of connection within me, not just to the mushrooms themselves but to the entire planet. It was as if these mushrooms had the power to awaken awareness, grounding people back into the natural world.

In recent years, my curiosity around liberty cap mushrooms has evolved from personal exploration to a keen interest in their medicinal potential. Research from institutions like University College London and the Imperial Centre for Psychedelic Research at Imperial College London has been incredibly inspiring. Having overcome depression myself, without the use of pharmaceutical drugs such as SSRIs, but through reconnecting with nature, energetic healing, and superfoods - I see this field as brimming with possibility. Over the years, I've witnessed the incredible transformations these mushrooms can offer, supporting individuals in ways that are often nothing short of remarkable and with no harmful side effects.

Healing Properties

Mental clarity, emotional healing, mood enhancement, alleviates depression, reduces anxiety, relief from PTSD symptoms, spiritual insight, neurogenesis, addiction treatment and enhanced creativity.

Anecdotal Evidence

Anecdotal evidence around liberty caps often centres on their psychoactive and transformative properties. Individuals who have worked with these mushrooms, particularly in controlled, ceremonial settings, report profound shifts in perception and consciousness. Many describe deep emotional healing and the dissolution of ego, allowing for a greater connection to nature, the self, and the cosmos. People struggling with depression, anxiety, or PTSD have shared how liberty caps helped them gain new insights into their conditions, often leading to a sense of peace, acceptance, and personal growth.

The psychedelic experience induced by liberty caps is frequently linked to feelings of interconnectedness with the earth and a reconnection with one's innate sense of purpose. These experiences, although they are highly subjective, have been transformative for many, often described as a pivotal moment in their development. As interest in the therapeutic use of psychedelics grows, stories of liberty caps helping individuals overcome mental health challenges and providing deep inner wisdom continue to emerge.

Scientific Research

Psilocybin and Mental Health
Psilocybin, the active compound in liberty cap mushrooms, has been studied for its potential to treat mental health conditions such as depression, anxiety, and PTSD. A landmark 2016 study conducted at Johns Hopkins University found that psilocybin, when administered in a controlled setting, significantly reduced symptoms of depression and anxiety in cancer patients. The effects were long-lasting, with participants reporting improved mood and well-being even six months after treatment.

[Study Reference: Griffiths, R. R., Johnson, M. W., & Carducci, M. A. Psilocybin for treatment-resistant depression. Journal of Psychopharmacology, 2016]

Neuroplasticity and Cognitive Function
A 2018 study published in Neuropharmacology demonstrated that psilocybin promotes neuroplasticity, the brain's ability to form new neural connections. Researchers found that psilocybin increased the growth of dendritic spines, which facilitate communication between neurons. This enhanced connectivity is believed to underlie psilocybin's potential to improve cognitive function and treat disorders like depression and anxiety.

[Study Reference: Ly, C., Greb, A. C., & Cameron, L. P. Psilocybin promotes neuroplasticity. Neuropharmacology, 2018]

PTSD and Trauma Recovery
A 2021 study at Imperial College London's Psychedelic Research Centre examined the effects of psilocybin on individuals with treatment-resistant PTSD. The results indicated that psilocybin therapy significantly reduced PTSD symptoms, suggesting that it helps individuals process and integrate traumatic experiences, leading to emotional healing.

[Study Reference: Carhart-Harris, R. L., Bolstridge, M., & Rucker, J. Psilocybin-assisted therapy for PTSD. Frontiers in Psychology, 2021]

Addiction Treatment

Liberty Cap mushrooms have also been explored as a treatment for addiction. A 2014 pilot study at the University of New Mexico found that psilocybin-assisted therapy helped individuals overcome nicotine addiction. After receiving psilocybin in a controlled therapeutic setting, 80% of participants remained abstinent from smoking six months later.

[Study Reference: Johnson, M. W., & Garcia-Romeu, A. Psilocybin for smoking cessation. Journal of Psychopharmacology, 2014]

Cluster Headache Relief

A 2017 study published in Cephalalgia investigated the effects of psilocybin on individuals suffering from cluster headaches. The study found that psilocybin helped reduce both the frequency and severity of headaches, providing relief for individuals who had not responded to conventional treatments.

[Study Reference: Sewell, R. A., Halpern, J. H., & Pope, H. G. Psilocybin for cluster headaches. Cephalalgia, 2017]

Additional Information

The active compound, psilocybin, is a prodrug that converts into psilocin in the body, which then binds to serotonin receptors in the brain, leading to altered perceptions, mood, and consciousness.

- **Psychological Benefits**: One of the most significant areas of research on psilocybin mushrooms is their potential to treat depression, anxiety, and PTSD. Clinical trials have shown that psilocybin-assisted therapy can lead to profound and lasting reductions in symptoms of depression and anxiety,

particularly in patients who have not responded to conventional treatments. A study published in *The New England Journal of Medicine* found that psilocybin was as effective as, if not more effective than, traditional antidepressants in treating major depressive disorder.
- **End-of-Life Anxiety**: Psilocybin has also been studied for its effects on patients with terminal illnesses, particularly in alleviating end-of-life anxiety. Research conducted at Johns Hopkins University and NYU Langone Medical Center found that a single dose of psilocybin significantly reduced anxiety and depression in terminal cancer patients, with effects lasting for several months.
- **Addiction Treatment**: Emerging research suggests that psilocybin may be effective in treating substance use disorders, including alcohol and nicotine addiction. A study published in *JAMA Psychiatry* reported that psilocybin-assisted therapy helped individuals with alcohol use disorder significantly reduce their drinking behaviour, with some achieving complete abstinence.
- **Neuroplasticity**: Psilocybin has been shown to promote neuroplasticity, the brain's ability to reorganise itself by forming new neural connections. This effect is believed to underlie the profound shifts in perspective and behaviour that many users experience, contributing to the therapeutic potential of psilocybin in treating various mental health conditions.

Additional Studies:
- **Carhart-Harris, R. L., et al. (2016).** "Psilocybin with psychological support for treatment-resistant depression: an open-label feasibility study." *The Lancet Psychiatry*, 3(7), 619-627.
- **Griffiths, R. R., et al. (2016).** "Psilocybin produces substantial and sustained decreases in depression and anxiety in patients

with life-threatening cancer: A randomised double-blind trial." *Journal of Psychopharmacology*, 30(12), 1181-1197.
- **Johnson, M. W., et al. (2014).** "Pilot study of the 5-HT2A receptor agonist psilocybin in the treatment of tobacco addiction." *Journal of Psychopharmacology*, 28(11), 983-992.

A Story of Success

Carl had severe PSTD from his time in military service. He'd had years of therapy and medical interventions that had given him little relief.

Internet research had led him to the potential benefits of micro-dosing liberty cap mushrooms.

As part of a trial he was able to obtain medicinal grade liberty cap mushrooms to take as a micro-dose under professional supervision. Within a month he noticed a significant difference and within 6 months his PTSD had gone.

How To Use

Because of current UK legislation, I cannot encourage the use of dried liberty cap mushrooms as they are a prohibited substance. One hopes that due to the enormous benefits of micro dosing liberty cap mushrooms, things change, and they become widely available for those who will benefit. To make a medicinal plant illegal, whilst allowing harmful alcohol and cigarette consumption baffles me!

Therefore, I cannot recommend you add them, in a careful dose, to your favourite herbal tea – and relax into a safe and spiritual space. Overconsumption of liberty cap mushrooms can lead to hallucinations, sickness and a 'bad trip'. If you are taking these mushrooms in a country where it is legal - be sensible. Respect the power of this mushroom. Even one fresh mushroom can lead you on a powerful journey! If you are taking liberty cap mushrooms in a dose beyond micro-dosing, it is recommended to take these mushrooms in a safe, therapeutic environment with support around you.

Featured Recipe - Raw Psilocybin Chocolate

Note: This recipe is only for those who live in countries where this mushrooms consumption is legal.

Creating a raw psilocybin chocolate is a way to blend the therapeutic benefits of cacao with the potentially transformative effects of psilocybin mushrooms. This recipe ensures that both the raw nature of the cacao and the delicate compounds in the mushrooms are preserved.
Here's a simple raw vegan recipe for making 10-15 psilocybin chocolates:

Ingredients:

- **10 grams of dried psilocybin mushrooms** (adjust depending on the strength you want per serving)
- **1/2 cup raw cacao powder**
- **1/4 cup cacao butter (melted gently)**
- **2 tbsp coconut oil (melted gently)**
- **2-3 tbsp maple syrup or coconut sugar (adjust for sweetness)**
- **1 tsp vanilla extract** (optional)
- **Pinch of sea salt**
- **Optional add-ins**: cacao nibs, shredded coconut, dried fruits, or adaptogens (like ashwagandha or maca)

Instructions:

1. **Prepare the mushrooms**:
     - Finely grind the dried psilocybin mushrooms using a coffee grinder or mortar and pestle until they are powdery. Set aside.
2. **Melt the fats**:
     - In a double boiler (or a heat-proof bowl over a pot of simmering water), gently melt the cacao butter and coconut oil together. Keep the temperature low to preserve the raw qualities of the ingredients.
3. **Mix the base**:
     - Remove the bowl from the heat and whisk in the raw cacao powder, vanilla extract, and sea salt. Stir until smooth and well-combined.
4. **Sweeten it**:
     - Gradually whisk in the maple syrup (or similar) tasting to adjust sweetness as you go.
5. **Incorporate the mushrooms**:
     - Once the chocolate mixture has cooled slightly (but is still liquid), gently fold in the powdered psilocybin mushrooms. It's important to ensure the mixture is not too hot, as high heat can degrade the psilocybin.
6. **Add optional ingredients**:
     - If you want to add any extras like cacao nibs or dried fruits, now is the time to fold them into the mixture.
7. **Pour and set**:
     - Pour the chocolate mixture into silicone moulds or a lined dish for easy removal. Spread it evenly.

8. **Chill and set:**
   - Place the moulds or dish into the refrigerator for at least 30 minutes, or until the chocolate has fully set.
9. **Cut or mould:**
   - Once set, remove the chocolate from the moulds or cut into desired portions.

Dosage Consideration:

- 10 grams of mushrooms into 10 pieces will means each piece contains 1 gram of dried psilocybin mushrooms. A micro-dose is between 0.2g and 1g.

Storage:

- Store your psilocybin chocolate in an airtight container in the refrigerator. It should last for several weeks.

Note: The effects of psilocybin vary based on individual tolerance, the users state of mind and the environment they are consumed in. If taking in a country where this is legal, always consume in a safe and mindful environment.

Warning: For those with schizoaffective disorder, a genetic history of mental health, or those with bipolar and other mental health conditions - only consume under medical supervision.

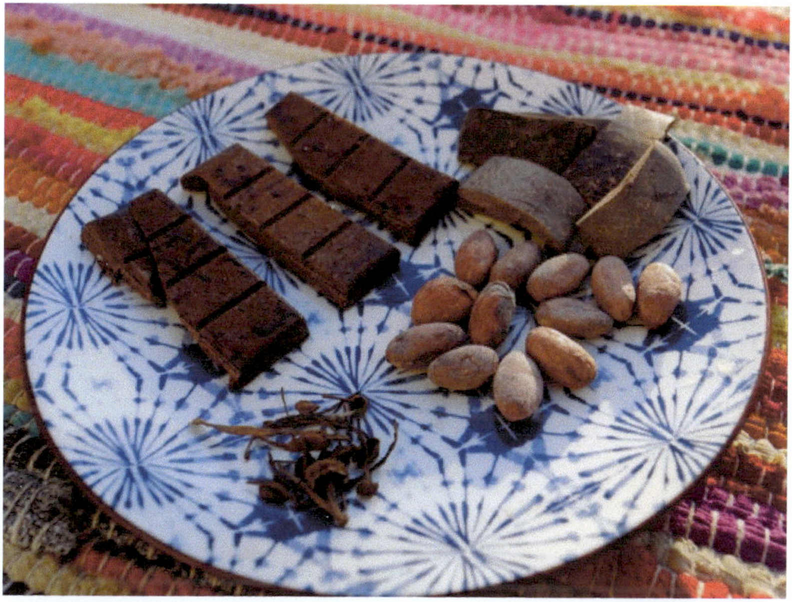

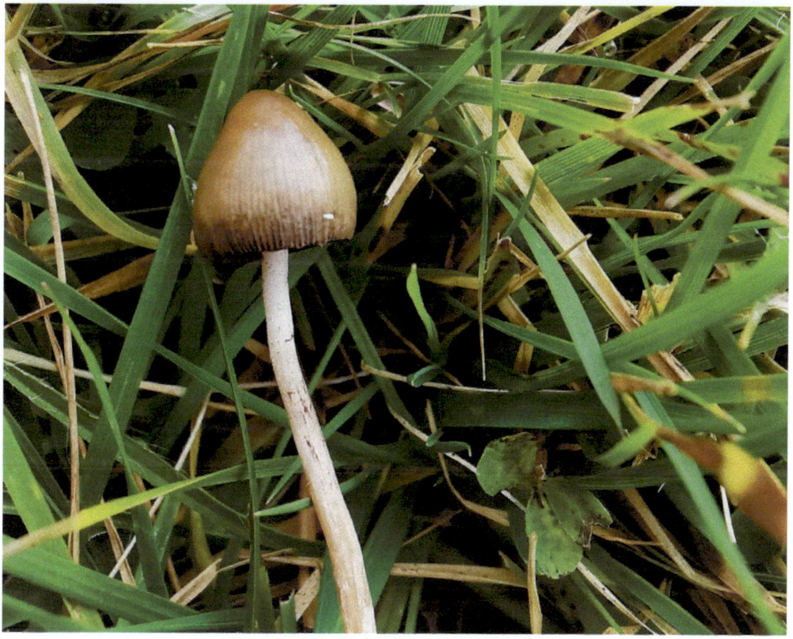

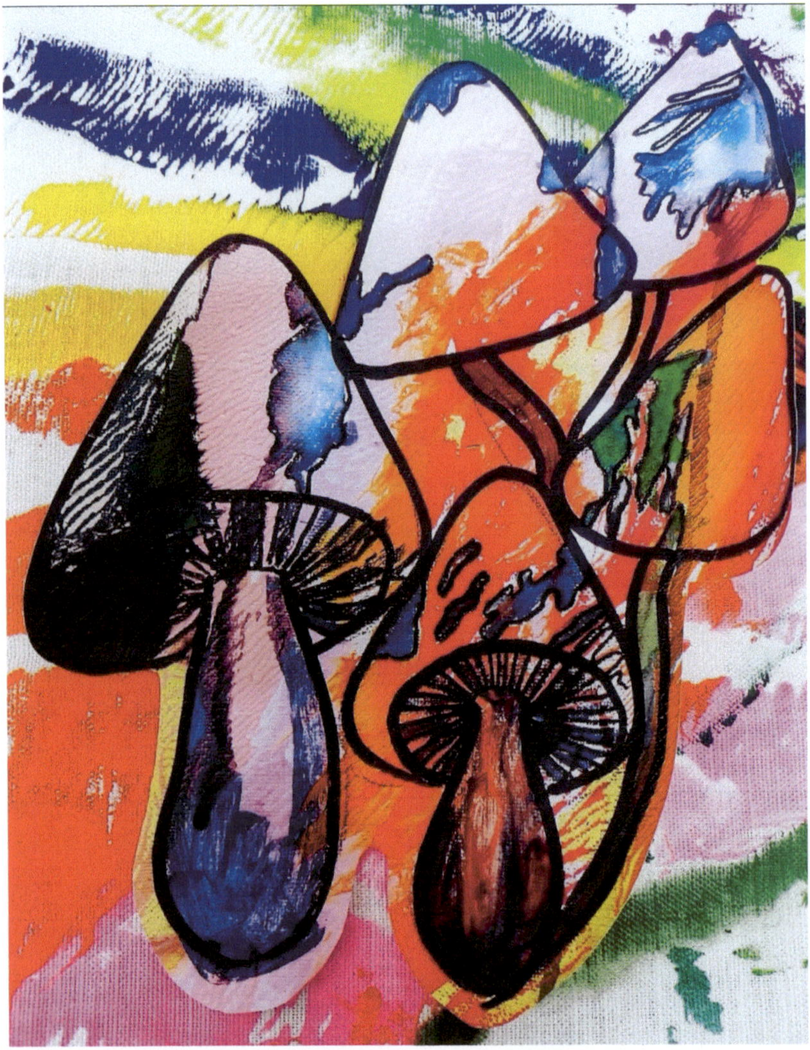

Fly Agaric
– The Fairy-Tale Mushroom

Other names – *Fly Mushroom, Soma, Pixie's Seat Mushroom, Fairy Tale Mushroom.*

Botanical – *Amanita muscaria*

The classic 'toadstool' from children's stories, this beautiful red and white spotted mushroom grows 8-14cm across and is mostly found in birch woods. It appears between August and December in groups. It is considered toxic, however there is evidence that in some cultures it has been prepared in a way to remove its toxicity.

Historical Use

Fly agaric has been known to induce strong hallucinations, visions and sometimes profound healing. One of the earliest recorded uses of fly agaric comes from Siberian shamanic traditions. The indigenous peoples of Siberia, including the Koryak and Chukchi tribes, used fly agaric in their spiritual rituals to induce altered states of consciousness. The shamans would consume the mushroom to enter a trance-like state, during which they believed they could communicate with the spirit world, predict the future, and perform healing ceremonies. It was also sometimes consumed by others under the guidance of the shaman to experience visions or gain spiritual insights. It has been said Siberian shamans would drink the urine (and sometimes meat) of the reindeer who consumed the mushroom, noticing how the animals appeared intoxicated. The reindeer would have purified some of the toxicity of the mushroom.

The story of shamans drinking reindeer urine might be partly allegorical. The head shaman of these tribes would sometimes be dressed in reindeer skins and antlers. The head shaman, through many years of purification rituals and developing inner resolve, had the power to consume the full dose. It may have been his urine that the students drank, as they would get a milder and less toxic dose.

As mentioned earlier, fly agaric is thought by some to have been an ingredient in the sacred Vedic drink Soma praised in 120 hymns of the Rig-Veda.

There is speculation that it was ingested before battle by the Berserker Viking warriors. This may have some truth as its active components have been found to inhibit fear in modern scientific research. It is also speculated to have been an ingredient in the witch's 'flying ointment' – allowing them to have visions and out-of-body experiences.

An artist's impression of a fly agaric shaman in 'flight'

In Northern European traditions, particularly among the Sámi people of Scandinavia, fly agaric was similarly used in shamanic practices. The mushroom's psychoactive properties, primarily due to compounds like muscimol and ibotenic acid, were utilized to induce visions and communicate with spirits.

In medieval times it was used as a fly catcher. It was placed in a saucer of milk, which the flies find very appealing. After feasting on it, the flies would become zonked out! Hence, its modern name - fly agaric - fly mushroom.

Folklore & Mythology

Fly agaric is steeped in folklore and mythology, particularly in Northern Europe. It is often associated with the figure of the shaman or wise person, who uses the mushroom to journey into the spirit world. In Siberian shamanism, fly agaric is believed to be a key to accessing other realms, and the red-capped mushroom is often depicted in traditional Siberian art and clothing.

In European fairy tales, fly agaric often appears as magical or even dangerous, representing the boundary between the natural and supernatural worlds. The mushroom is frequently depicted in stories and art as a symbol of mystery, transformation, and the unknown.

Fly agaric is also connected to the concept of the "fairy ring," a naturally occurring circle of mushrooms that was believed to be the site of fairy gatherings or portals to other realms. Fly agaric is seen as both a guide and a guardian to these mystical places.

One of the most enduring myths surrounding fly agaric is its connection to the legend of Santa Claus. Some historians and ethnomycologists suggest that the modern image of Santa Claus, with his red suit and white fur trim, was influenced by the red and white colours of fly agaric. The theory suggests that reindeer, which are native to the regions where fly agaric is found, may have consumed the mushrooms, leading to the myth of flying reindeer. Additionally, the idea of Santa Claus descending through chimneys could be linked to the shamanic practice of drying fly agaric mushrooms on the branches of trees or near the hearth, which visually resembles the decoration of Christmas trees.

My Story with Fly Agaric

Fly agaric has always held a sense of mystique for me, being the mushroom of fairy tales and folklore. My journey with this mushroom, however, has been quite different from others, as I've never taken it internally. I have learned that we can connect with the spirit of plants and mushrooms without physical consumption. The fly agaric is one such being whose spirit I have journeyed with deeply, without the need to ingest it.

This mushroom brings forth the spirit of dreaming, offering pathways to connect with ancestors and dive into the mysteries of the earth and cosmos. I have often sat in meditation, focusing on an image of fly agaric, allowing its deep, dream-like essence to envelop me. This journey led me to research more about its history and uses, guiding me to the traditions of Siberia, where shamans and doctors have long revered fly agaric for its remarkable ability to relieve pain and release trauma, particularly stored in the fascia of the body.

The realization that this mushroom affects the fascia intrigued me, as it began to reveal a profound truth: the fascia of the human body shares similarities with the mycelium network of mushrooms. It felt as though fly agaric was showing me that we, too, are part of a larger, interconnected mycelium-like web, one that binds us to all living things.

Healing Properties

Pain relief, trauma release, fascia healing, nervous system support, anti-inflammatory, spiritual connection, sleep aid, dream enhancement, mood regulation and ancestral healing.

Anecdotal evidence

The use of fly agaric in modern times is somewhat niche but still prevalent among certain groups, particularly those interested in shamanic practices, ethnobotany, and psychoactive experiences. Anecdotal reports of fly agaric use vary widely, reflecting the mushroom's complex and unpredictable effects.

Many users describe the experience of fly agaric as profoundly spiritual, with vivid dream-like visions and a deep sense of connection to nature or the cosmos. Some compare it to lucid dreaming, where one can navigate the experience with a degree of control, while others report intense, uncontrollable hallucinations.

Fly agaric is also sometimes used for its sedative properties. Some users take it in small doses to promote relaxation and sleep, although this is generally not recommended due to the mushroom's potential toxicity.

There is much anecdotal evidence of its use to treat pain and heal physical trauma in the body when used topically. When used in this way it is non-psychoactive.

There are numerous reports of negative experiences, including nausea, vomiting, confusion, and prolonged delirium. These accounts highlight the importance of proper preparation and dosage when using fly agaric, as well as the potential risks involved.

Scientific Research

Pain Relief and Trauma Release
Fly agaric has been traditionally used in Siberian shamanic practices for its pain-relieving properties. A 2015 ethnopharmacological study revealed that compounds in fly agaric act on the central nervous system, reducing pain and inflammation. The study also noted its potential for releasing trauma stored in the fascia, a concept supported by traditional Siberian medicine.

[Study Reference: Ratsch, C., & Müller-Ebeling, C. The pain-relieving properties of Amanita muscaria. Journal of Ethnopharmacology, 2015]

Dreaming and Sleep Enhancement
Fly agaric is often associated with dream enhancement and altered states of consciousness. A 2018 study published in Psychopharmacology explored the effects of muscimol, the active compound in fly agaric, on sleep cycles. The study found that muscimol increased slow-wave sleep, the deepest phase of sleep, which is associated with memory consolidation and physical recovery.

[Study Reference: Russo, E. B., & McKenna, D. J. Muscimol's effects on sleep. Psychopharmacology, 2018]

Anti-inflammatory and Antioxidant Effects
A 2020 study found that fly agaric contains antioxidants and anti-inflammatory compounds that may reduce inflammation in the body. The study revealed that fly agaric extracts lowered markers of inflammation in animal models, suggesting potential applications in treating chronic inflammatory conditions such as arthritis.

[Study Reference: Shulgina, T., & Korshunova, Y. Anti-inflammatory properties of Amanita muscaria. International Journal of Medicinal Mushrooms, 2020]

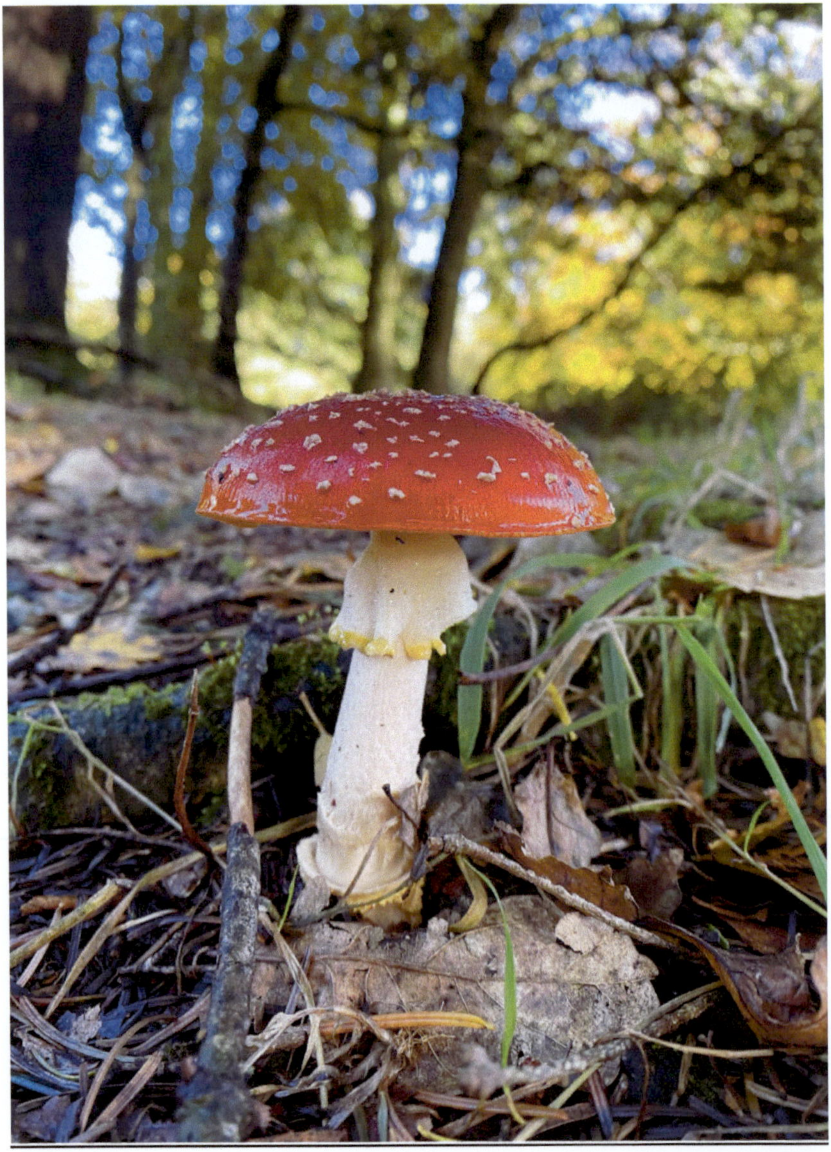

Neuroprotection and Cognitive Enhancement
Fly agaric has been studied for its potential neuroprotective effects. A 2019 study found that muscimol, one of its primary active compounds, exhibits neuroprotective properties by modulating GABA receptors in the brain. This action helps protect neurons from damage and could offer benefits for cognitive function, particularly in neurodegenerative conditions.

[Study Reference: Petroff, O. A. C., & Stafstrom, C. E. Neuroprotective effects of muscimol. Neuropharmacology, 2019]

Trauma and Fascia Connection
Fly agaric has been used traditionally to release trauma stored in the fascia of the body. A 2022 study suggested that fly agaric's ability to modulate the central nervous system could promote the release of physical tension and emotional trauma, aligning with Siberian shamanic practices.

[Study Reference: Popov, A., & Kharitonova, A. Trauma release with Amanita muscaria in traditional medicine. Journal of Ethnobiology, 2022]

Additional Information
Scientific interest in fly agaric primarily revolves around its psychoactive properties and the compounds responsible for these effects - muscimol and ibotenic acid. Unlike psilocybin mushrooms, fly agaric induces a different kind of psychoactive experience, often described as dream-like, sedative, and sometimes delirious.

Psychoactive Compounds:
The primary active compounds in fly agaric are muscimol and ibotenic acid. Ibotenic acid is a prodrug that converts into muscimol upon decarboxylation, which occurs when the mushroom is dried or heated. Muscimol is a potent GABA receptor agonist, which means it mimics the action of the neurotransmitter GABA, leading to sedative and

hallucinogenic effects. These effects can include altered perceptions of time, vivid visual and auditory hallucinations, and a sense of euphoria or spiritual insight.

Neuropharmacology:
Research on the neuropharmacology of fly agaric has provided insights into how muscimol and ibotenic acid interact with the brain. Muscimol's ability to cross the blood-brain barrier and bind to GABA receptors explains its powerful psychoactive effects. A study published in the Journal of Neurochemistry detailed how muscimol modulates GABAergic transmission, leading to altered states of consciousness.

Toxicology:
Despite its traditional use, fly agaric is considered toxic and should be approached with caution. The mushroom can cause a range of symptoms, from mild euphoria to severe nausea, vomiting, and delirium. Cases of poisoning have been documented, particularly when the mushroom is consumed raw or in large quantities. However, traditional preparation methods, such as drying or parboiling, can reduce its toxicity.

Potential Therapeutic Uses:
Although fly agaric is primarily known for its psychoactive effects, some studies have explored its potential therapeutic applications. Research published in the Journal of Ethnopharmacology suggests that muscimol might have neuroprotective effects, possibly offering benefits in the treatment of certain neurological disorders, though more research is needed in this area.

Additional Studies:
Bowden, J. H., & Drysdale, A. C. (2001). "The psychoactive constituents of Amanita muscaria." Journal of Neurochemistry, 75(6), 199-210.

Michelot, D., & Melendez-Howell, L. M. (2003). "Amanita muscaria: Chemistry, biology, toxicology, and ethnomycology." Mycological Research, 107(2), 131-146.

Yoshimura, H., et al. (1998). "Neuroprotective effects of muscimol from Amanita muscaria in animal models." Journal of Ethnopharmacology, 64(3), 191-198.

A Success Story

Don is a roofer, who has had the misfortune to have fallen off 4 roofs, leaving him with severe aches and pains. A friend have him a balm made with fly agaric mushroom and other healing herbs. As a test, he applied it to one of his injured arms. Within 10 minutes the pain had gone. He proceeded to spread it all over his aching body, bringing him great relief.

How To Use

Fly agaric's two components, ibotenic acid and muscimol, are responsible for its psychoactive and hallucinogenic effects. To minimise its toxic side effects, fly agaric would be processed in some way - either dried, made into a drink, smoked or made into ointments. The preparation of this mushroom, and of the person receiving it was vitally important. Legend tells how the Celtic Druids would purify themselves by fasting and meditating for three days, drinking only water before consuming it. The Saami chief shaman who consumed it similarly did so after fasting.

Note: Fly agaric should not be consumed unless done with expert supervision and knowledge. This is not something to mess around with.

Featured Recipe - Fly Agaric Pain Balm

Creating a Fly Agaric Pain Balm requires careful preparation. The psychoactive compounds should be handled with respect and care. When used externally it is not psychoactive and has traditionally been used for pain relief, especially for issues related to the fascia, joints, and muscles. This is a recipe from a Siberian shaman.

Note: This recipe is for historical purposes only and not intended to be made in any country where this is illegal.

Fly Agaric Pain Balm

Ingredients:

- 1 cup dried fly agaric mushroom caps, broken into small pieces (avoid using the stems)

- 1 cup olive oil (or any carrier oil like coconut oil, almond oil, or jojoba oil)
- 1/4 cup beeswax/candelilla wax (for a solid balm; adjust for desired firmness)
- Essential oils (optional, for scent and extra therapeutic properties, such as lavender, frankincense and copabia)
- Clean glass jar for storage

Instructions:

Infusing the Oil:

1. **Prepare the Mushroom Caps:**
   - Break the dried fly agaric mushroom caps into small pieces.
   - Place the pieces in a clean, dry jar.
2. **Infuse the Oil:**
   - Pour the olive oil (or your preferred carrier oil) over the mushroom pieces until they are fully submerged.
   - **Slow Method:** Seal the jar and leave it in a warm, dark place to infuse for 4-6 weeks, shaking the jar occasionally.
   - **Quick Method:** If you're short on time, you can use a double boiler. Place the jar in a pot of water over low heat, ensuring the water doesn't boil. Let the oil gently infuse for 4-6 hours. Stir occasionally to make sure the mushrooms are fully immersed in the oil.
3. **Strain the Oil:**
   - Once the infusion is complete, strain the oil through a fine mesh sieve or cheesecloth, making sure to squeeze out all the oil from the mushrooms. Discard the mushroom pieces.

- Store the infused oil in a clean jar for further use or proceed to make the balm.

Making the Balm:

1. **Melt the wax:**
   - In a double boiler, gently melt the beeswax / candelilla wax over low heat until fully liquified.
2. **Add the Infused Oil:**
   - Slowly add the Fly Agaric-infused oil to the melted wax, stirring constantly. Mix until the wax and oil are fully combined.
3. **Add Essential Oils (Optional):**
   - If desired, add 5-10 drops of essential oils to the mixture for added therapeutic effects or a pleasant aroma. Lavender and frankincense are good choices for pain relief and relaxation.
4. **Pour and Cool:**
   - Carefully pour the mixture into a clean jar or tin while it is still liquid.
   - Let it cool and solidify completely at room temperature.
5. **Store and Use:**
   - Store the balm in a cool, dark place. It should last for several months.
   - **Application:** Apply a small amount to the affected area, massaging it gently into the skin. This balm is intended for external use only.

124

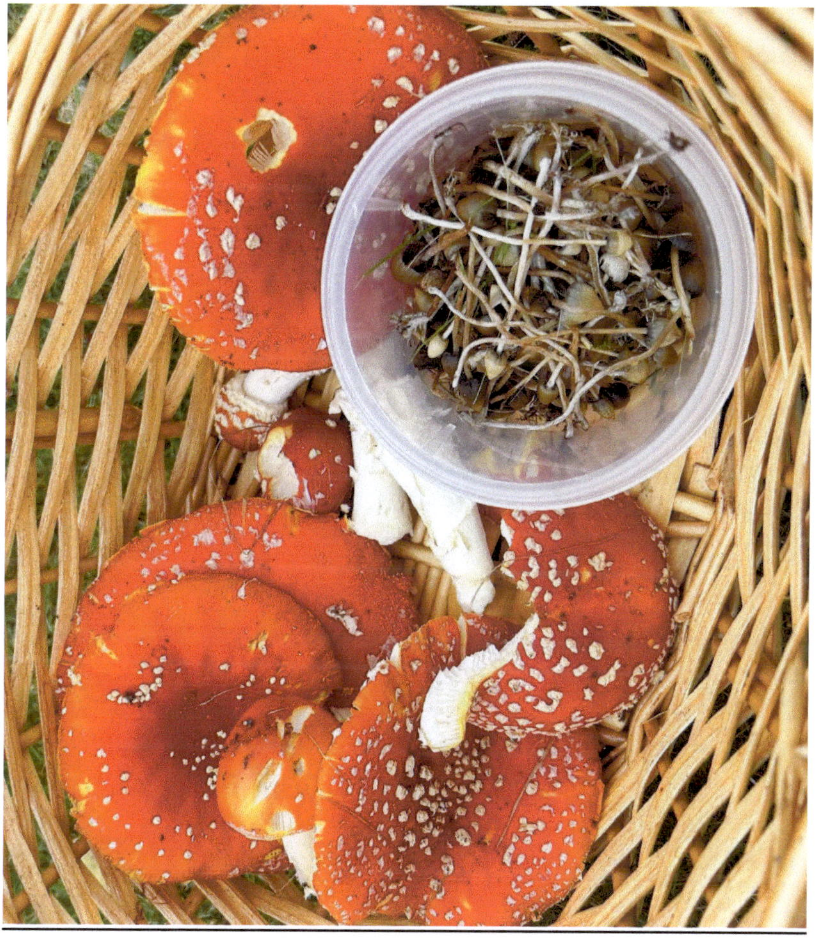

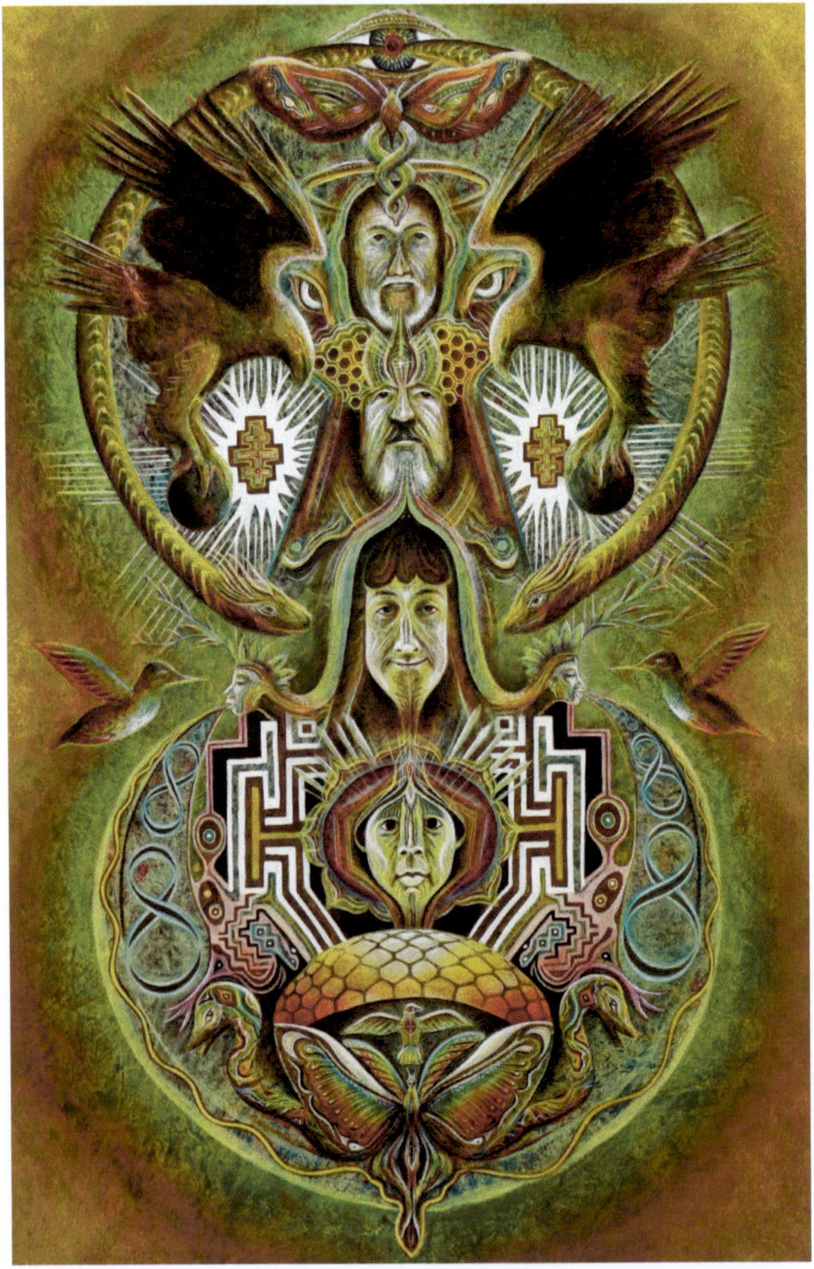

Afterword

A Mycelium Meditation by Giles Bryant

Oh, mycelium.....
How your great white firmament
Spreads across the world
Like a network of light
Under oceans, beneath concrete cities, through desserts.

How you connect all species
Like a great Internet of nature.
But unlike the computer version
You are self-powered and non-polluting.

You spread communication
Between trees and plants.
So that if one is in need
You communicate the message
That brings help and assistance.

You guide all species
To work in symbiosis.
Showing co-operation is more effective
Than the competitive ways of Darwin's Folly.

Oh mycelium....
You are the thread that empowers the fruits
That have inspired this journey
Through these 7 magical mushrooms.
You give birth to chaga, reishi
lion's mane, turkey tail
liberty cap & fly agaric

May we heed the call
Of the connection you display
And realise, like you
We are all connected. We are one.

Mushroom love to you all!

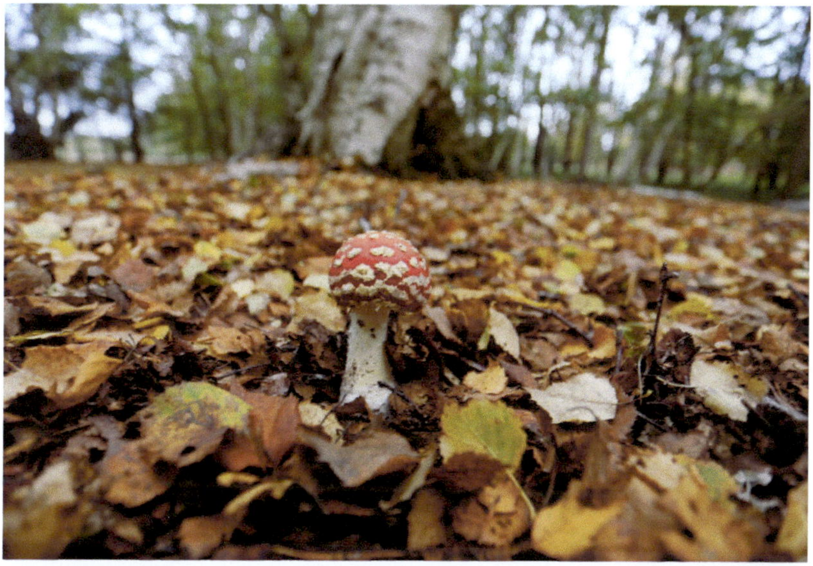

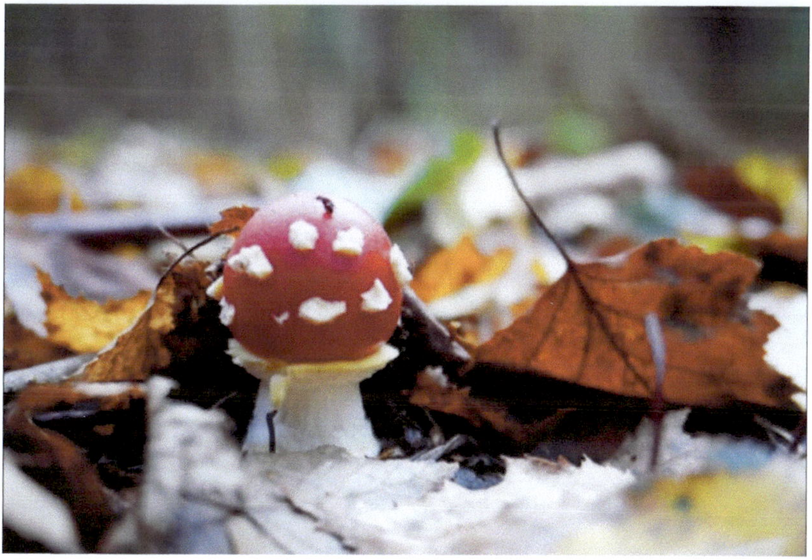

Bibliography

Allegro, John M. *The Sacred Mushroom and the Cross: A Study of the Nature and Origins of Christianity Within the Fertility Cults of the Ancient Near East.* Doubleday, 1970.

Bryant, Juliette. *Superfoods and How to Use Them.* Juliette's Kitchen Press, 2017.

Dann, Geoff. *Edible Mushrooms: A Forager's Guide to the Wild Fungi of Britain, Ireland and Europe.* Green Books, 2016.

Gillam, Fred. *Poisonous Plants in Great Britain.* Wooden Books, 2008.

Hanford, Robin. *Edible and Medicinal Wild Plants of Britain and Ireland.* Createspace Independent Publishing Platform, 2017.

Hobbs, Christopher. *Medicinal Mushrooms: An Exploration of Tradition, Healing, & Culture.* Botanica Press, 1995.

Letcher, Andy. *Shroom: A Cultural History of the Magic Mushroom.* Ecco, 2008.

Paterson, Jacqueline. *Tree Wisdom: The Definitive Guidebook to the Myth, Folklore and Healing Power of Trees.* Thorsons, 1996.

Phillips, Roger. *Mushrooms.* Macmillan, 1981.

Powell, Martin. *Medicinal Mushrooms: A Clinical Guide.* Mycology Press, 2012.

Powell, Martin. *Medicinal Mushrooms: The Essential Guide.* Mycology Press, 2010.

Knight, Peter & Sue Wallace. *Albion Dreamtime.* Stoneseeker Press, 2019.

Schultes, Richard Evans, and Albert Hofmann. *Plants of the Gods: Their Sacred, Healing, and Hallucinogenic Powers.* Updated Edition by Rätsch, Christian. Healing Arts Press, 1992.

Seed SistAs. *Poison Prescriptions: Power Plants for Magical and Medicinal Use.* Aeon Books, 2021.

Sheldrake, Merlin. *Entangled Life: How Fungi Make Our Worlds, Change Our Minds & Shape Our Futures.* Random House, 2020.

Stamets, Paul. *Mycelium Running: How Mushrooms Can Help Save the World.* Ten Speed Press, 2005.

Stamets, Paul. *Psilocybin Mushrooms of the World: An Identification Guide.* Ten Speed Press, 1996.

Street, Chris. Earthstars: The Visionary Landscape. Hermitage Publishing, 2000.

Wasson, R. Gordon, and Valentina Pavlovna Wasson. *Mushrooms, Russia and History.* Pantheon Books, 1957.

Wolfe, David. *Chaga: King of the Medicinal Mushrooms.* North Atlantic Books, 2012.

Wolfe, David. *Superfoods: The Food and Medicine of the Future.* North Atlantic Books, 2009.

Wolfe, David. *Longevity Now: A Comprehensive Approach to Healthy Hormones, Detoxification, Super Immunity, Reversing Calcification, and Total Rejuvenation.* North Atlantic Books, 2013.

Wright, John. *The Forager's Calendar: A Seasonal Guide to Nature's Wild Harvests.* Profile Books, 2019.

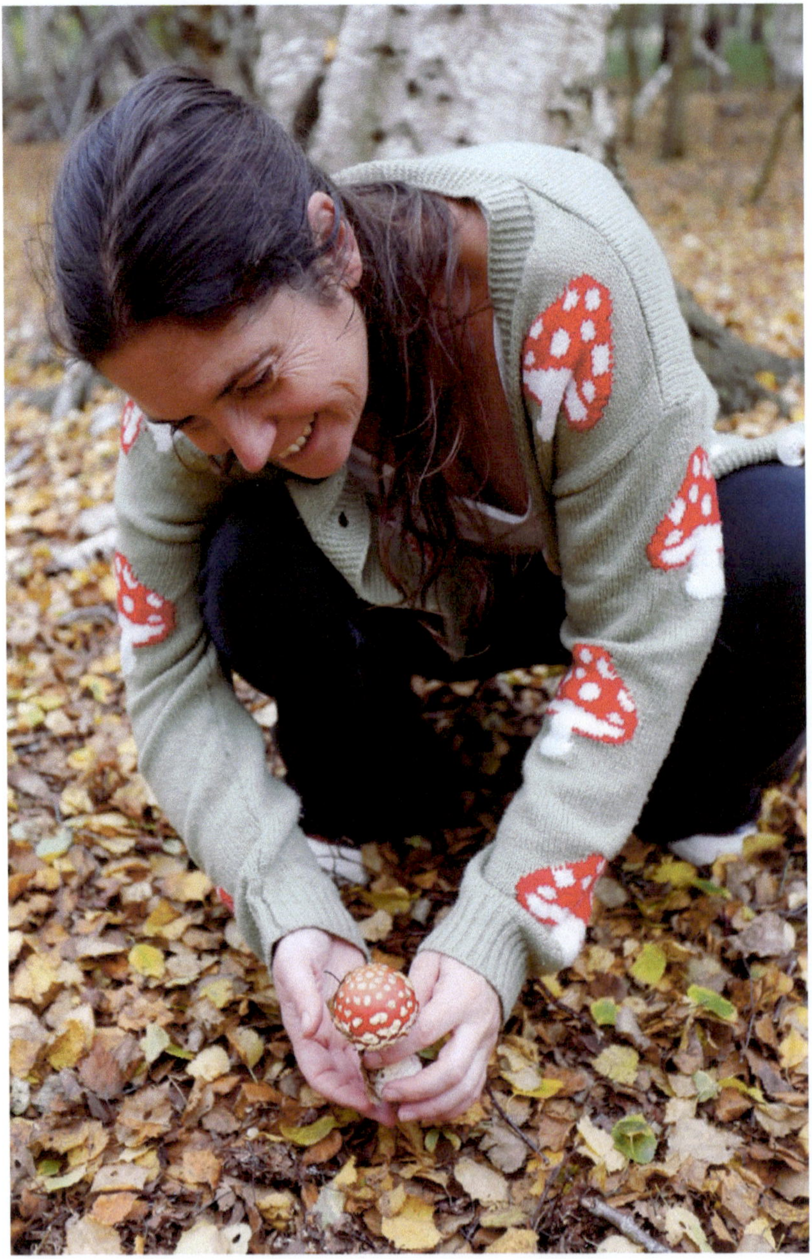

About The Author

Juliette Bryant is a renowned wellbeing expert, author, and educator with a deep-rooted passion for natural health and the transformative power of plants. Her life's work centres around helping people reconnect with the healing wisdom of the earth through practical and nourishing approaches to all-round health. As well as *7 Magical Mushrooms* she is the author of *Divine Detox*, *Divine Desserts*, and *Superfoods and How to Use Them*, which together offer readers a comprehensive guide to embracing nature's bounty for physical and emotional wellbeing.

Beyond her books, Juliette is a nutritional consultant, superfood alchemist, and earth wisdom keeper, passionately sharing her knowledge through her wide range of superfood products, retreats, workshops, and educational programs that inspire others to live in harmony with the natural world. Through her work, she guides people on the journey to vibrant health, demonstrating how plants, mushrooms, and nature's resources can be potent allies in creating a balanced, healthy life.

Through her writings, teachings and personal example, Juliette is an unwavering advocate for sustainable living and deep earth-based wisdom. Her work is infused with a reverence for nature's intelligence and a heartfelt commitment to helping others unlock their innate potential for wellness, healing, and transformation.

Juliette is married with 3 boys and lives in beautiful rural Suffolk in England where she runs Juliette's Kitchen – a superfood company with the motto: "Make delicious food your medincine."

www.juliettebryant.com

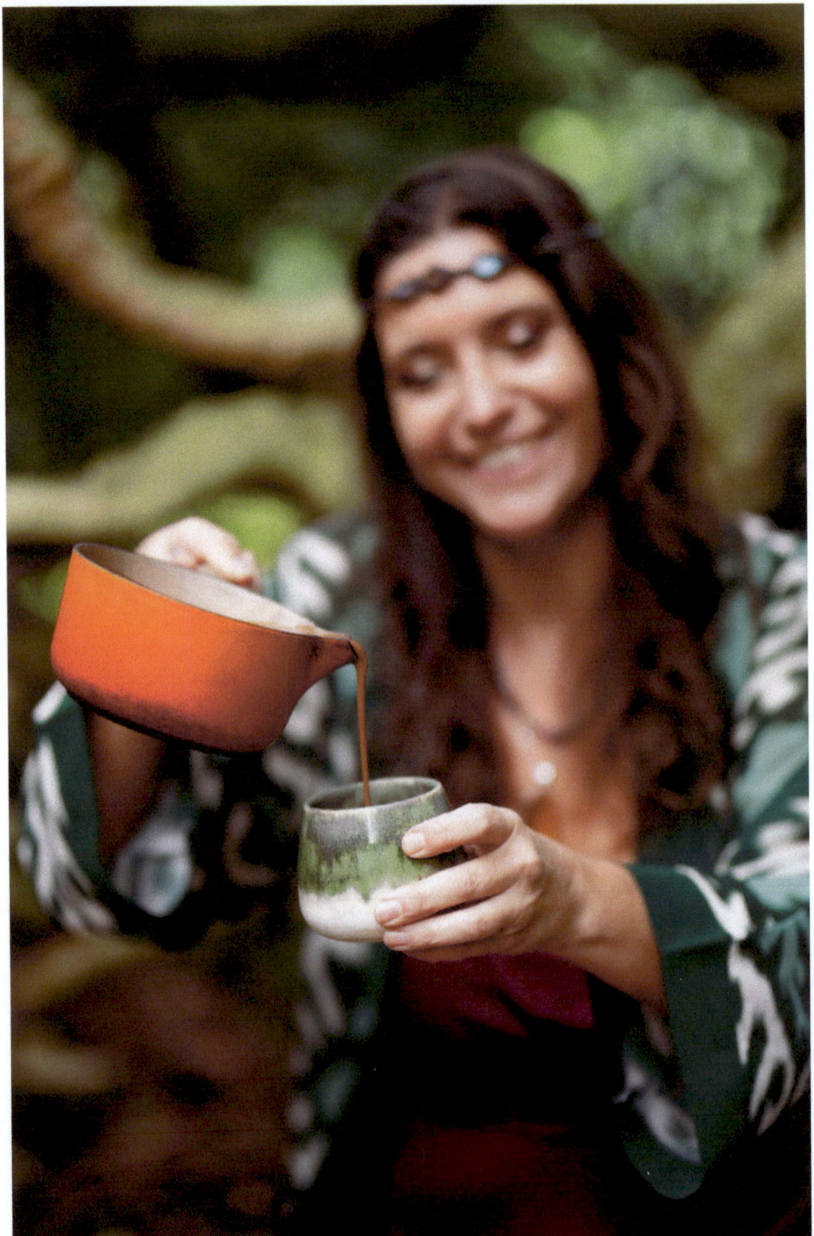

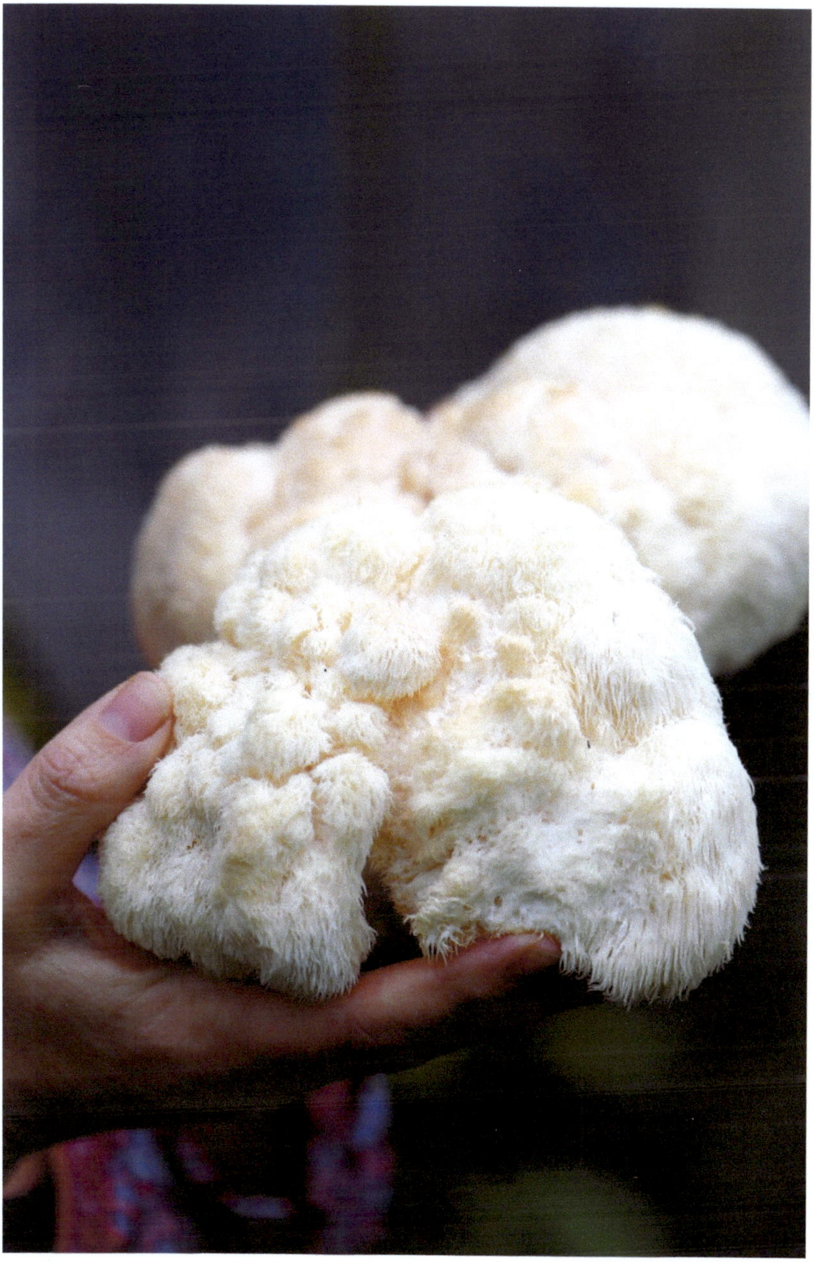

NOTES